16 METHODS OF
GROUP BIBLE STUDY

William Metcalf

16 METHODS OF GROUP BIBLE STUDY

Judson Press ® Valley Forge

16 METHODS OF GROUP BIBLE STUDY

Unless otherwise indicated, Bible quotations are from *The New English Bible,* second edition © 1970 by
permission of Oxford and Cambridge University Presses.

Other versions quoted in this book are:
  Authorised Version (AV) This version is very similar to the King James Version.
  Revised Standard Version (RSV)
  Good News Bible (GNB)

Library of Congress Catalog Number 79-89268

ISBN 0-8170-0856-X

Printed in the United States of America

The name JUDSON PRESS is registered as a trademark in the U.S. Patent Office. Printed in the U.S.A.

CONTENTS

	Introduction	7
1	Reading the Bible	9
2	The Activity Approach	25
3	Line-by-Line Study	38
4	Quizzes	53
5	Study through Subjects	67
6	True-to-Life Studies	80
7	Exposition and Discussion	88

16 Methods of Bible Study

1.	Extended Readings	10
2.	Imaginative Reading	14
3.	Prepared Individual Reading	16
4.	United Readings	21
5.	Playlets	25
6.	Group Role-Plays	27
7.	Formal Dialogue	30
8.	Visuals	32
9.	Debates	35
10.	Line-by-Line Study	38
11.	Quizzes	53
12.	Intellectual Subjects	69
13.	Devotional Subjects	74
14.	Creative Subjects	77
15.	True-to-Life Studies	80
16.	Exposition and Discussion	88

Introduction

Frequent reference is made in this book to 'conventional Bible study'. The context will usually be found to be critical, but is nowhere intended to be derogatory. The phrase is used here to describe that kind of group study which consists basically of exposition by one person, perhaps followed by discussion. Because this is probably the most common formula for study, it may be described as conventional. It is an authentic and effective way of studying, and, as the last chapter of this book will suggest, may even be the most durable way of coming to regular grips with Scripture.

Even so, it does not deserve the monopoly it enjoys, because it is by no means the only way to study together, and may be an unsatisfactory way for many modern Christians, at least as an introduction. It sets a premium on the ability to discuss and to listen to purely verbal exposition, and these techniques are by no means at everyone's disposal. There are other ways to a man's awareness – music, art, drama, reading, current affairs, hymns – and any one of these may attract and hold his essential interest where other methods have failed. We can deplore the average congregation's apathy towards the midweek Bible study, and can mourn over its lack of interest in 'spiritual things'. But we must at least concede that the fault is just as likely to lie in the form in which we have chosen to present the living Word. In general terms, indifference to Bible study can have only a few root causes – the words studied are weak and irrelevant, or the people do not really want to study, or the presentation of the Word to the people is unattractive. This book offers a constructive examination of the third possibility.

What follows, therefore, is not a series of arguments in favour of a new approach, but a variety of practical alternatives at the disposal of leaders who are already aware of the need for change. Most of the suggestions given have already been carried through in quite a variety of study situations, with sufficient apparent success to warrant this documentation. Where it has been thought necessary, details of content and procedure are given; in other cases, only the direction in which experiment is possible has been indicated. The ideas have mainly been personally developed, and none is knowingly borrowed from any printed source. At the same time, originality has not been a prime aim; it seemed better to amass as many ideas as possible, to convince the study leader that the whole world is his oyster when it comes to enlisting educational technique in the service of Bible study.

Here and there it has proved impossible not to interlace this collection of practical ideas with words and thoughts which betray the excitement of spiritual experiment. Having fully acknowledged the need to *com*prehend the message and content of Scripture, I inevitably return to the conviction that spiritual truth is essentially *app*rehended by something other than the intellect. If in fact we are 'transformed by the renewing of the mind', then the intellect, the need to think, has a greater place in Christian worship and service than is usually accorded it. Yet it remains only an avenue to that part of man which moulds his attitudes, inclines his will, and really *knows* his God. When that kind of knowing takes place in the context of Bible study, there is good reason for excitement, and I do not mind getting lyrical about it.

1
Reading the Bible

One of the odd things about many group Bible studies is that in them the Bible itself is often unread, except in a cursory way. At most, the passage will be read once by the leader or in a 'round the room one verse per person' style, then the time is given over to exposition and discussion. In such circumstances, the manner of reading is bound to suffer. People tend to read in a halting, colourless way, because the exercise requires neither the intensity of a personal reading aloud on one's own, nor the tone and projection of a public reading.

Other disadvantages follow, perhaps unnoticed. There is often a great deal of mis-reading, as people lose the place, or unfamiliar proper nouns loom up to drain one's confidence, or less efficient readers take over. In the deepest sense, this doesn't matter – truth remains truth. Yet the reading cannot be said to have helped the study in general. Then again, there can sometimes be an air of boredom about reading familiar passages, even if they are well loved, and a 'here we go again' feeling can be subconsciously present, affecting the attitude to later study.

Another constant feature about such reading, which may be thought desirable as well as inevitable, is its seriousness. The words are taken at their face value, and it is assumed that they must be said seriously because they come from a serious source, as it were. If there is any other emotion present in the reading, it is usually the quiver of devotion and gratitude in the voices of the group elders, or the fervour in the trained voice of the preacher. The fact is that such reading, rightful as it is, predisposes the group to adopt a quiet, pious approach to the study that follows.

So, casual Bible reading, even if only a formality, has a real influence on the mood of the study to come. This chapter, however, concerns itself with ways in which different, more imaginative reading of Scripture could bring about responses in people not possible with the standard approach. To accept this suggestion with anything like sympathy, two premises must first be approved.

1. The reading of Scripture can have study and inspirational value on its own, as an end in itself, quite apart from the value of discussion and research. If we say that the Bible is inspired in a unique way, it could follow that we might get more from soaking ourselves in those inspired words than from our far from inspired discussion about them. We have not sufficiently explored the power of the Bible, *just as it stands*, to work its own way in people willing to let it.

2. The accepted ways of reading Scripture aloud do less than justice to it. If there is humour in the Bible, which can hardly be doubted, our invariable solemnity effectively disguises the fact. Its poetry has no chance against our prosaic reading. Even its intensity and zeal have to conform to our decorum. At the very least, we must concede that (a) the mood in which Scripture was written has little in common with the manner in which it is now read; and (b) it would be desirable to at least try to restore that original mood in our study, if not in our worship.

Consider one or two ways in which this attempt can be made.

Extended Readings   1

This simply means allowing time to read far longer extracts at one sitting. One could have, in effect, a Bible *reading* group rather than a Bible *study* group. The two could happily combine, however, as it is surprising how much Scripture can be read in a short time if the reading is uninterrupted. For example, the six chapters of Galatians would take about twenty-five minutes, even with indifferent readers. To start a Bible reading programme with a pastoral letter would immediately illustrate one of the chief benefits of this method. To read a scriptural letter from beginning to end – no preamble, no background data – would be to accord it, probably for the first time on the part of most readers, the respect we unthinkingly give to our personal, much less consequential mail. Most letters only make sense if read right through, especially if they are seeking to develop a line of thought, and biblical letters, being in this sense only a literary form, can be no exception.

So read a letter through and notice:

1) how your assessment of the writer alters, for better or worse, as you follow him through the *whole* of what he wanted to say, doctrinally or personally.

2) how the reality of the letter seems to increase. The people greeted are authentic people, the problems dealt with can be seen to arise out of life situations, the ethics preached have a clear relation to the doctrine that has gone before.

3) how well-known texts, phrases or passages slot themselves into a continuous whole. Soon they will no longer be seen as contrived, other-worldly statements for preachers to talk about, evangelists to wield, calendar compilers to recommend. They are high spots in an otherwise ordinary letter, when the writer, having tried to express his thoughts more than once, finally finds strong, beautiful words which time has proved to be memorable and lasting.

4) how such texts often come to have a more accurate meaning to the reader. The remark will often be made after group reading, 'So that's where the text comes in! Ah, and I see now what it means!' The text has finally been visited in its own home, as it were.

5) how the words themselves are liberated. For instance, in the case of the letter to the Galatians, more than one reader will notice for the first time how humorous (even indelicate, if we take polite Western conversation as our norm) Paul is when he says about some of his pro-circumcision detractors, 'As for these agitators, they had better go the whole way and make eunuchs of themselves!' (Gal. 5:12); or how satirical when he refers to

Peter and James as 'those reputed pillars of our society' (Gal. 2:9). In another vein, whoever is reading when chapter 3 verse 1 comes round, will surely by now, out of new understanding, put far more feeling into 'you stupid Galatians!' than does the average preacher when he *starts* with this verse in the Sunday lesson.

6) finally, how the group as a whole feels a distinct sense of achievement. Whatever may or may not transpire in the study to follow, reading the letter was a thing in itself. It was a kind of vigil, a happening. It is not uncommon for a reading group to go on and on through the months, steadily reading letters, gospels, prophecies; its members building up their own cross-reference system from memory as they see how themes recur and are variously treated. Nor is it uncommon for lifelong Christians to be driven to say, at the end of concentrated reading of exciting Scripture, 'If this is right, then we are wrong!' And this fear, of course, is the beginning of wisdom.

Obviously, variants on the basic extended reading method are possible, and are listed here as a guide.

1. Continuous reading can be the sole function of the group, with only a brief sharing of one's reflections to end each session.
2. It can be the introduction to a study, or a series of studies, along conventional lines.
3. Reading can be basically continuous and devotional, with the understanding that the individual is free to interrupt the reading whenever he wishes to discuss a point, clear up a doubtful meaning, etc.
4. Full use can be made of the new translations and paraphrases. A most rewarding time is promised, for instance, to those who persevere in the group reading of J. B. Phillips's *Four Prophets*.

Finally, one or two technical suggestions about this simplest of methods:

1. It requires no leader, either in deciding the next book to be read, or the way in which each book is read. In this respect it is easy to organise, and allows established leaders the pleasure of enjoying study without having to initiate it!

2. Generally, reading should not be regimented. Reading round a group in turn has practical snags known only too well to sufferers, and sets up psychological barriers less well known. People have been known to stop attending altogether because of the fear of having to take part when their turn comes. It is better to suggest that people should read —

– AS MUCH AS THEY WANT TO! This gives good readers the human pleasure of giving their voice an extended work-out over a paragraph or two. It allows the poorer readers, or the reserved person, to join in only when ready (it will happen!). Eventually, as the reading gains momentum, there will be good-natured jockeying for position, as people set their sights on favourite extracts! This will often mean spontaneous duets or trios, the unforced beginning of choric work, and the pleasure of such occasions will be self-evident to speakers and listeners.

– HOW THEY WANT TO! This is important. From the first, and throughout (someone will need to keep reminding the group about this), it should be made clear that readers may adopt any mood which fits either themselves or the material they are reading. All sorts of options are open. There is the normal style, already described, which will soon get less and less popular as groups gain experience. Or paragraphs can be read in a conversational, chatty way. Then there is the oratorical style, large and aggressive; the dramatic style (people have been known to add gestures and movement, almost without knowing it); assorted moods – anger, penitence, sorrow, humour. All this helps to bring the words to life and prepare for any follow-up study.

3. Do trust the Bible to work its own way. Assuming the group to be interested in the idea to begin with, there is no need to top-and-tail the reading with prepared talks, considerations of date, destination, authorship, etc. This need to trust the living Word cannot be stressed too much, for those wishing to approach Bible study in a new way.

Wordsworth was not exaggerating when he persuaded,

> One moment now may give us more
> Than fifty years of reason.

It is possible to argue that a man who is granted a moment of real insight into Scripture can learn more about that one truth than he could arrive at after a hundred academic attempts. For example, set a young man down on the floor, imagining himself as the lame man at the Beautiful Gate (Acts 3:1–10). Then invite other members of the group to go over to him and say, as Peter did, 'In the name of Jesus Christ of Nazareth, walk.' Let the young man get up as commanded, but *only* when he senses a kind of power in the speaker – in his voice, his eyes, his bearing – which could make him believe, even for a moment, in the possibility of such a miracle. He might wait for a long time, and for many speakers, as each sheds his flaccid, predictable delivery and tries to think his way back into the marvellous moment. Provided people are willing to at least try losing their self-consciousness, there awaits for them, especially for the man on the floor and the man who eventually lifts him, an apprehension of the mystery of miracles such as a lifetime of sermons might not give.

In one Bible study like this people were asked to say, 'My God, why hast thou forsaken me?' as they imagined Christ said it on the cross. Forewarned, none used the measured, calm tones of the pulpit; all put what they could into the experience, with widely differing results. It was left to one man to bring the group as close as it was to get to a reality which it recognised. He had gone briefly out of the room, returning with his arms entwined behind him around a gnarled branch he had seen lying outside the conference centre. In real pain, he took quite a time before attempting the line, and when it came it was *wrenched* from him.

Obviously, the best scriptural material for this kind of approach will be first-person readings. The basic method is to take well-known texts and read them in such a way as to re-create the context. Gesture and movement are not necessary to the method, though a conditioned group will eventually add these automatically. Here are a few more ideas.

1. Let someone attempt Psalm 51:1–13, perhaps on his knees.
2. Still in penitential mood, try Luke 15:11f. (the prodigal).
3. Have fun with the variety of expression offered for 'Almost thou persuadest me to be a Christian' (Acts 26:28AV). This text should evoke speedy recourse to other translations, to try to determine Agrippa's original inflection.
4. Someone can read short extracts from Paul's letters to one other member of the group, at dictation speed, so reliving the situations in which Paul wrote (e.g. 2 Tim. 4:7–18).
5. Rather more ambitiously, someone can read extracts from Peter's sermon at Pentecost (Acts 2:14f.) or the end of Stephen's apology (Acts 7:44f.), both to heckling accompaniment supplied by the rest of the group! If entered into seriously, this will tell the group a lot about the writer's choice of words, the tradition and thinking of the Jews, the offence of the Gospel.
6. A creative tension can result from someone taking a paragraph of the words of Jesus, or an incident from his life, and reading the passage in the second person, that is, replacing the words 'Jesus' or 'he' with 'you', and making other grammatical adjustments where necessary. This would have the effect of bringing Christ into the group, as it were, and of compelling readers to consider whether they really accept the challenge of what he said and did. Think, for example, of the difference if we read the last part of one of the miracle accounts (Mark 9:26–29) as follows:

... the boy looked like a corpse; in fact, many said, 'He is dead.' But you took his hand and raised him to his feet, and he stood up. Then you went indoors, and they asked you privately, 'Why could not we cast it out?' You said, 'There is no means of casting out this sort but prayer.'

When such source ideas fail, try things the other way round.

Reflect on situations which cause us to speak in certain ways, and fit a Bible passage to this mood.

1. A formal style of speaking, as if giving witness in court or making a press release. e.g. Paul before Felix (Acts 24:10–21); Peter before the council (Acts 11:5–17).

2. Orations. Plenty of material here – the sermons of Peter, Paul, Stephen; Paul's farewell speeches (Acts 20:18–35); Moses's (Deut. 32); Joshua's (Josh. 24:2–23).

3. Excited accounts, that is, accounts in which the speaker himself gets excited. Several of the above passages can be treated like this, and there are also such incidents as Christ's appearance on the Emmaus road (Luke 24), the miracle stories, etc. (These are in the third person, and would be related as if a bystander were breathlessly reporting the happenings to a group of friends, or perhaps cynics.)

4. Narration in newscaster style, e.g. accounts of the day of Pentecost, the crucifixion, etc.

5. As if the reader can hardly restrain his laughter, e.g. some of the accounts of Jesus' dealings with the Pharisees when he confounded their questions.

6. The halting, shocked tone of a survivor of a disaster, e.g. Paul's shipwreck, Paul and Silas in prison.

Prepared Individual Reading 3

Obviously, some of the foregoing ideas will be the better for some preparation. This raises the larger question of how far Bible study can be enhanced by a group member coming ready to present the reading under discussion. It is arguable that such a feature, rarely likely to take more than five minutes if presented properly, could grace a study as a devotional highlight, quite apart from whatever real contribution it makes to the actual study.

Before arguing the case further, consider the following suggestions.

1. A straight, well-delivered reading can be pointed by suitable

musical backing, either live, if there is a competent instrumentalist in the group, or recorded. Some of Paul's great doctrinal flights almost need majestic, soaring music to complete them; the gentler sections of John's letters would be further softened by quiet string music. The process can be reversed by playing some mood music, then asking people what kind of Scripture comes into their minds at the sound of it.

2. Taped readings are worth the effort involved if a special effect is aimed at (though rarely otherwise). The words of Christ (especially the high-priestly prayer of John 17), or passages such as God's reply to Job (Job 38f.) could have special meaning if played to a group sitting without books, even with eyes closed. (Try putting the tape-recorder outside the room, with increased volume.) In other words, when a sense of remoteness or 'otherness' is wanted, the tape-recorder comes into its own.

3. Occasionally, the passage under consideration is echoed in popular hymns or gospel songs, in which case an obvious variant would be to introduce the reading along with the songs it has inspired. This idea, in turn, leads on to the larger question of:

4. Anthologies. There are several ways in which individuals or small groups can present the reading along with other material, so as to directly contribute to the study value of the class:

a) by presenting the chosen passage in a series of parallel readings from various translations. This could mean reading the same passage several times in turn, but it is probably better to interleave one basic translation with variants of particular phrases. The result would be a kind of home produced Amplified Bible, and would save a lot of searching about for alternative translations during the discussion afterwards.

b) by interleaving the passage, not with parallel translations, but with other sections of Scripture which help to illustrate or explain the passage under study. For example, Christians like to ascribe the description of the Suffering Servant in Isaiah 53 to Jesus Christ. Assuming this to be the passage for study, two readers could introduce it as follows (in this and the following example I have used the RSV):

He had no form or comeliness . . .

Can anything good come out of Nazareth?

and no beauty that we should desire him.

'Then what shall I do with Jesus who is called Christ?' They all said, 'Let him be crucified.'

He was despised . . .

Is not this the carpenter's son? Is not his mother called Mary?

and rejected by men . . .

All the city came out to meet Jesus; and when they saw him they begged him to leave their neighbourhood.

a man of sorrows . . .

And taking with him Peter and the two sons of Zebedee, he began to be sorrowful and troubled. Then he said to them, 'My soul is very sorrowful, even unto death.'

and acquainted with grief . . .

Jesus wept. When he saw the city of Jerusalem he wept over it.

and as one from whom men hide their faces.

Another maid saw Peter, and she said to the bystanders, 'This man was with Jesus of Nazareth.' And again he denied it with an oath.

c) by illustrating Scripture with relevant quotations from literature in general, so offering a starting point for discussion. Take, for example, the much used introduction to the Gospel of John:

In the beginning was the Word . . .

[John] is seeking common ground with his readers . . . he wants a term that carries thought nearer to the heart of all reality . . . The Jew will remember that 'by the Word of the Lord were the heavens made'; the Greek will think of the rational principle of which all natural laws are particular expressions. Both will agree that this Logos is the starting-point of all things.　　　William Temple

. . . and the Word was with God, and the Word was God.

Truth is not truth in that exacting land [India] unless there go with it kindness and more kindness and kindness again, unless the Word that was with God also is God. And the girl's sacrifice ... was rightly rejected, because, though it came from her heart, it did not include her heart.   E. M. Forster

In him was life, and the life was the light of men. The light shines in the darkness, and the darkness has not overcome it.
The darkness in no sense at all received the light; yet the light shone still undimmed. So strange is the relation of the light of God's revelation to the world which exists to be the medium of that revelation.   William Temple

The true light that enlightens every man was coming into the world.
                              One, spirit. His
Who wore the plaited thorns, with bleeding brows
Rules universal nature.   William Cowper.

I think, therefore, that the purpose and cause of the incarnation was that He might illuminate the world by His wisdom and excite it to the love of Himself.   Peter Abelard

And the Word became flesh and dwelt among us ...
Flesh is the ideal medium of self-expression. That is why God chose it ... We humans understand nothing until it is made flesh ... The Word was made flesh — soft flesh, warm flesh, live flesh that throbbed and felt and developed and matured, as all sound and healthy flesh will.   F. W. Boreham

... full of grace and truth.
Jesus not only disclosed the divine reality, but therein also displayed its beauty. Truth is august, often austere, sometimes repellent. But here it is gracious and winning.
                              William Temple

d) by the less artistic but perhaps more penetrating method of piercing Scripture with headlines and quotes from the daily newspaper which contradict the Bible's claims and promises.

One has only to think of such huge statements as those in Romans 8 ('in everything [God] co-operates for good'; 'there is nothing . . . in all creation that can separate us from the love of God'), and the 'dailies' leap to the challenge.

It will be agreed that this kind of introduction needs preparation, and could well be entrusted to individuals other than the over-all leader. However, the leader should have a fair idea of what to expect, and even more of what use he is going to make of the varied and thought-provoking material which will be presented.

The biggest advantage of this method, quite above that of varying the content of the class, is the way it allows other abilities and flairs to be used purposefully yet naturally in Bible study. One of the big weaknesses of conventional study-discussions is that they set too high a premium on talents which people do not normally have in abundance – the abilities to study and discuss! These are techniques, and people who have not mastered them cannot express themselves to advantage if they are the only ones being adopted. Many intelligent, knowledgeable men and women shy away from midweek studies because they feel their limitations when it comes to articulating their thoughts in words. Let the same people be allowed to choose their own expression medium, and the sensitivity and understanding thought to be lacking may well be unearthed immediately.

So, if a musician finds that his music as well as his power of abstract thought is equally welcome in Bible study, he may join the group more often. The same could be said for the actor, the reader, the painter, the photographer, the modeller, the collector (the very mention of these interests should have sparked off other ideas of introducing the Bible passage!). Each of these enthusiasts has as much right to exercise his talent as the natural debater.

There is practical difficulty in furthering this democratic ideal, and one of a perverse nature. Having succeeded in arousing a man's interest in Scripture through his other interests, a leader often finds himself having to restrain the enthusiasm aroused! Otherwise, as the old story has it, the camel may end up in the tent with the man outside. A visual aid specialist may have the

happy idea of introducing the parable under discussion by showing a film-strip while the passage is being read, but it turns out
that it takes him half the class period to erect the equipment! A
musician may have found some admirable music, but insists, on
aesthetic grounds, that the whole of the symphony should be
played! Leaders should resist such innocent take-over bids, and
insist that all the media chosen, including debate, are only the
'handmaid of Piety', not the eventual master.

United Readings 4

This description covers far more than the familiar reading
together of Scripture, or its more elaborate presentation in choric
style. Both techniques are valuable, and should be used where
the material to be read calls for it. It is possible, however, to go
beyond this kind of group work to activity which calls for
rather more imagination, and certainly some degree of libera-
tion. It may be better to wait until the group has reached a place
where the members are well known to each other *as group members,* and where experimentation is accepted as the norm. On the
other hand, the following exercises could help to bring about
such a desirable state. The important thing is to realise that not
all groups respond to, or even like, self-conscious activity. For
one thing, it often deteriorates (or ascends?) into hilarity, an
emotion normally suspect in Bible reading circles. Then, too, it
can cause embarrassment to reserved individuals, though it will
be the embarrassment born of inadequacy and not unseemliness.
The fact is that spontaneous group readings test the imagination
of the members, and where that imagination is not strong, or has
not been used much in the past, there is likely to be a negative
reaction. The leader will soon find out! With this as with all
slightly startling techniques, he is always open to the easy charge
of using gimmickry, innovation for the sake of it. And to be fair,
he himself must make sure that he rightly divides between
gimmickry and that kind of experiment which he knows to be
purposeful and rightly directed.

The suggestions are these.

1. Refer back to the section on imaginative reading and arrange similar situations requiring group rather than individual reactions. Let the group be the apostles praying with fearful boldness (Acts 4:24–30); the mob shouting 'Crucify him!'; the disciples saying, 'Is it I?'; the Jews praising God for deliverance (e.g. Psalm 106). They should not say these passages chorically, that is, in a disciplined, synchronised way. Each member should have his personally selected way of saying them, and should say them that way while everyone else is saying them another way! If even a small group of believers were asked to read again in silence Galatians 2:20 ('I have been crucified with Christ . . .'), then say each phrase out aloud only after he has again absorbed its heart meaning for himself, there could be no thought of everyone finishing at the same time. And if the group waited in silence until the last man or woman had finished, that silence would speak volumes.

2. It will be well known that one feature of Jewish poetry was its balancing of thoughts rather than sounds. This often made for verses clearly divided into two, with contrasts or comparisons in each part: e.g.

For the Lord KNOWS the *way* of the **righteous**,
but the *way;* of the **wicked** will PERISH. (RSV)

Such structures are particularly found, of course, in many of the Psalms, and sections of Job and Proverbs. Study of an appropriate section can be introduced by inviting the group to look briefly over the passage, and select only the key words, contrast or comparison, which they personally wish to stress by reading. They can choose a different contrast in each verse, or can decide to emphasise the same feature throughout, e.g. concentrating on verbs ('knows . . . perish') or nouns ('righteous . . . wicked'), etc. They should be further encouraged to say each word as they want to, with whatever emphasis, volume, change of pitch, etc. they like. It is as if each member is working out his own pattern of meaning from the whole, seeing the power of particular contrasts for himself. To give this kind of reading pace and coherence, one designated person reads the whole of the passage quietly and without expression, allowing everyone else to chime in with the words they have chosen to read. If the exercise is undertaken seriously, good discussion will follow, as some members are bound to have seen new inflections of meaning.

3. Choose passages, including some mentioned above, which divide easily into short, simple sentences. Let each member in turn read one sentence, which is immediately echoed by the whole group. The individual tries to introduce some original or at least distinctive expression into his reading; the group tries to copy his style, pitch, intonation, volume, etc., as closely as possible. The greater the attempt to reproduce the original reader, the more likelihood there is of the rest coming to a new and sharp understanding of the text. (Conversely, lack-lustre attempts are next to useless as study aids.) This is one area in which the gifted reader can use his ability on behalf of the group, as he can help others to hear the inflections of meaning which they would not have identified themselves.

4. A variant of this method is to take a text of any kind, providing it has value in itself, and see in how many different ways it can be spoken. Again, the whole group can echo individual attempts, and the individual should insist on repeating his interpretation until he is satisfied that the group has copied him correctly. No possible interpretation should be ignored—flippant, bored, pessimistic, excited, etc. — simply because it does not appear to be in keeping. We have probably programmed ourselves too much to expect certain stock interpretations of texts, simply because they are 'religious', and the whole spur to this kind of experiment is the hope of stumbling upon new truth.

Sample sentences or phrases would include:

I can do all things through Christ. (Phil. 4:13AV)
I am not as other men. (Luke 18:11AV)
My son, God will provide (Gen. 22:8AV)

5. This next suggestion could well be regarded as a kind of game. Certainly, it can occasion much laughter. The idea is for a leader to have certain *exaggerated* renderings of a particular passage in mind, then try to get the group to reproduce his ideas *without actually speaking himself*. He can use gesture, facial expression, movement, but he cannot put words into their mouths. As with some parlour games, he can pre-arrange signals which indicate that the group should all return to the beginning of a sentence to try again, or that a particular member has latched on to the 'right' interpretation and should therefore be copied by the rest. When the passage has thus been laboriously and hilariously worked through, it is read again in entirety, as some kind of final performance, incorporating all the interpretations striven for.

The obvious point of the exaggeration is to help people to see the beauty of the original. A supreme example of this is the imagery of Isaiah, the largeness of which is lost in our prosaic reading. By him we are assured that, thanks to the excellency of God, 'the parched ground shall become a pool' (35:7AV). If our dumb leader stands with hands grasping throat, tongue lolling, he *may* induce the group to say 'pa.a.a.a.r.r.ched' as if they *were* parched, spiritually desiccated, shrivelled. For 'pool', the leader needs gestures which soothe and satisfy, an expression of rest and certainty, because he really wants to hear 'poo.o.o.o.o.l.l.l' from the group, as if at last rain had fallen on their dusty souls. Isaiah had painted vivid pictures in the first place, and we are only trying to recapture their vividness.

One can imagine the inherent dangers of the method. It has the seeds of indiscipline, burlesque, irreverence. It may be a long time before all the group responds to such flank attacks on their real interest and involvement. The fact remains that one flash of spiritual imagination can short-circuit its way to that 'understanding of the heart' which is our final goal. This possibility seems to justify using the reading of Scripture, in its own right, in as many sincere ways as possible.

2
The Activity Approach

If it is accepted that the possibilities of imaginative reading can be explored in the cause of Bible study, it is only an extension of the same principle to include man's other natural expression aids – gesture and movement. Without further argument, therefore, here is a cluster of suggestions for approaching Scripture through dramatic activity. It is admitted that if these ideas are put into practice, the practical result would not be a Bible study in the accepted sense of the phrase, but rather a Bible-based activity evening. Yet there would be many worshippers who would welcome the change!

Playlets 5

This is an obvious place to start, because we have a long tradition of reliving biblical incidents in simple dramatic form, and it will be sufficient to list the possible variations:
1. Keeping only to the actual words of the Bible, the characters act out their parts, while a narrator fills in the rest. The parts can be learnt, or read.
2. The whole action can be mimed to the words spoken by a narrator.
3. As a variant of (2) the narration can be pre-recorded.
4. Individuals can attempt narrative readings, adding personal interpretative movement to the words.
5. Without straying as yet from the basic text, the various methods already mentioned can be repeated using paraphrases. This could simply mean taking two or three alternative

translations and using them together, varying the delivery of each. In the case of individual readings there are now available in print many interesting paraphrases, such as modern versions of the parables, in dialect or colloquial form.

There is quite another form of straight playlet which has been the 'bread and butter' of religious drama for years. That is what we might call biblical fiction. It is the technique of taking biblical characters and attributing them with motives, histories, relationships, etc., for which there is no specific warrant in Scripture, with the intention of moralising on the message of Scripture. In such plays, for instance, Matthew's son turns out to be the boy with the loaves and fishes, and his neighbour is the woman healed of an issue of blood – hence his willingness to follow Christ on sight. In such plots, Judas is credited with as many motives for betraying Christ as there are plays about him. We all know the pattern, and have probably been grateful for such plays at one time or another.

To this genre we can add the more literary results of the imagination, such as the soliloquies in Clive Sansom's *The Witnesses* and the popular David Kossoff paraphrases. Then there are the more disciplined dramatic readings of J. B. Phillips in *A Man Called Jesus*.

For *study* purposes, any use of the prepared playlet or dialogue should include making an important distinction between the kinds of fiction in the material. Strictly speaking, any fact or observation not mentioned in the original text is imaginary, and may therefore be false, so far as Scripture is concerned. If false, subsequent study may be built on false premises. But there are degrees of falseness. Inventing imaginary connections between Bible characters for the sake of dramatic neatness and effect; speculating on motives; attributing characters with statements and opinions for dramatic effect – these are all acceptable on the stage, but not to the student who is trying to evaluate the authentic background of Scripture.

On the other hand, Scripture will often make a brief statement and leave it unadorned. In such cases it is possible to speculate on the implications of the statement. We know, for instance, that although Christ healed ten lepers at one time only one returned to give thanks, and there is the strong implication that the episode is recorded to illustrate ingratitude. One can therefore speculate, with Christ, 'Where are the nine?' In *Wrestling with Christ*, Luigi Santucci comes up with an imaginative answer. Three were celebrating their cleansing at the inn, one was back to his lechery, one was hiding behind a bush waiting to rob a house he had been 'casing' while leprous, one was again driving a hard bargain over the purchase of an ox, one was too proud to return, one had just forgotten, and one had contracted leprosy again from his girl because he hadn't wanted to be healed (therefore separated from her) in the first place! Now a student of human nature can evaluate this list to see if this is the kind of thing that people do with their freedom. There are still no grounds for claiming any one excuse as factual, but the Bible did say that nine people did not return, and we may recognise this particular explanation as *authentic* even if not factual. As such, it therefore has a place in Bible study, in much the same way as we use devotional commentaries to help understand the significance of what Scripture does not actually say except by implication.

If this point is accepted, it allows a look at other ways in which the spontaneous playlet can be used in serious Bible study.

Group Role-Plays   6

Sometimes it is desirable to attempt a re-creation of a Bible situation as authentically as possible. An illustration will serve to make the point. Persuade the group, or part of the group, to be the church at Colossae, waiting for the arrival of Paul's letter. The cast should comprise the people actually mentioned in the letter, plus people holding the particular points of view defended or attacked in the letter. The narrative should closely reflect the content, the aim being to demonstrate that this letter, like all letters, was written to real people with developed characters. In the case of Colossians, the cast list would read something like this:

Philemon (consult Col. 4:9. The actor should also read the
      letter to Philemon)
Nympha (4:15)
Archippus (4:17)
A slave (3:22)
A master (4:1)
Someone following practices suggested in 2:18
Someone holding views suggested in 2:4
Tychicus (4:7)
Onesimus (4:9)
At least one person who already holds the views Paul is going
to expound in the letter.

Perhaps the value of this method would be better illustrated
if more detailed case notes were set out for those who were going
to prepare themselves for the roles. If one attempted to recon-
struct a 'pre-letter' conversation in one of the Galatian churches,
for instance, the following cast would at least be needed:

A Judaizer. This type of man is the main cause of disturbance.
He casts doubt upon the authority of Paul (Gal. 1:11f.), as being
secondhand (1:17). This Paul has cheapened the Gospel by deny-
ing the need for circumcision and therefore obedience to the
Mosaic Law (1:10). The Judaizer may be motivated by fear,
because how can a man know he is saved if all his external
landmarks – rules, symbols, etc. – are dispensed with? Paul
suggests such men are jealous (4:17-20) and afraid of persecution
(6:11-13).

A pagan convert, wavering in her faith because of the influence
of the Judaizers (4:8-11). She had only known pagan gods and
rites and was afraid of displeasing them. There was something to
be said for having special days to observe and rituals to perform.

A 'freedom-lover', who couldn't see what all the fuss was about.
This free religion is marvellous (5:13-21). No rules! The Christian was free to do what he liked (5:23). No exacting command-
ments, no yearly trips to Jerusalem (2:1). There is grace to cover
sin, so why not sin? To this man Christianity is an undisciplined

faith; released from rules the pendulum has swung the other way for him.

A man 'endowed with the Spirit' (6:1). This man sees both sides of the argument and gently shows the error in thinking on either side. He could remind the others of their first contacts with Paul and Christ (4:12–16; Acts 13:1–16:6) and the experiences they had had (3:2, 4–5). Was this all the result of law or faith? He argues that pagan ritual bears no comparison with the peace that was found in Christ; that the law of love is higher than the law of fear (4:7). He admits the inherent dangers in the freedom offered in Christ, and is adamant that this is a freedom to love (5:14), not to gratify self.

The study value of such detailed role-plays as this should be obvious, as group members come to grips with the issues of Scripture as they reveal themselves in the attitudes of people. There will be the immediate value of making sense of written material by putting it all back into direct speech. In spontaneous acting of this kind, people can only say what is meaningful to themselves, and it will soon be evident whether or not they have grasped the issues. There will be all the potential humour of acting out other people, and the inevitable addition of anachronisms, modern punch-lines and local references which may appear at times to take the whole exercise into the realm of farce. In a real sense, however, such a development may be a better indication of success than a sincere, laboured performance.

On the other hand, there will be times when the leader will know that a particular group member is no longer acting, but is trying to grapple with his own problem through the safe medium of another character. There will be members of modern congregations who have never been able to strike the right balance with regard to this 'freedom thing', and are still bound either to a fearful observance of tradition and form, or to a fatal licence of thought and conduct which discourages them even as they indulge in it. At such times, if the leader is looking for this kind of *ultimate* value from his studies, the play acting could cease, and the action would pass naturally into a real, almost crucial discussion of the heresies which still linger on in every congregation. Role-plays have been known to become earnest dialogues between two people, while others sat breathlessly around, knowing that Galatia, for instance, was now far away.

> And lo, Christ walking on the water,
> Not of Gennesareth, but Thames!

Of course, to see such results groups must submit themselves to the disciplines of the role-play technique, and these disciplines may be studied in the appropriate manuals. In principle, however, the role-play idea can be used to re-create all kinds of scriptural situations: the individual churches (as illustrated), the Council at Jerusalem (Acts 15), the deliberations of the Sanhedrin (Acts 5:27–39), etc. In each case the study purposes will be:

1) To master the content of the original Scripture and reproduce it faithfully in direct, modern, imaginative speech.

2) To follow through any devotional or study problem thrown up in the acting process.

Formal Dialogue 7

The role-play idea can be varied slightly to bring about a more formal, perhaps therefore more studious, result. This variation requires two members to be relatively well informed about the subject they tackle, because the essence of the exercise is for the rest of the group to listen and learn.

For instance, it is possible to get a lot of study benefit from that part of Galatians which might well be passed over in the ordinary way, namely, the autobiographical section (1:13–2:14). This section can be approached by putting Paul in the dock, that is, to ask one member to read the passage carefully, master its details, and then submit himself to formal questioning on it as if he were Paul himself speaking. The scene could be as in a courtroom, with whatever embellishments one liked. The onus of making this a learning exercise would of course fall on the interrogator. He would need to be asking three kinds of questions:

1) those which could be answered out of a full knowledge of the Scripture in question, e.g.

How long did you stay with Peter on your first visit to Jerusalem? (Gal. 1:18)

Why was pressure put on you to have Titus circumcised? (2:3-4)

After your conversion, did you go immediately to Arabia? (1:17)

2) those which cannot be answered from Scripture, but which the interviewee replies to out of his own view of Paul, and the total impression gained from the letters in general:

Did you *enjoy* persecuting the Christians before your own conversion?

What was your personal relationship with Peter?

Why did you not undergo instruction from experienced Christians before going off into solitude?

3) those which could not be answered from that particular part of Scripture, but which involve other Scripture, or could be answered with some authority given sufficient background knowledge. For instance, 'How do you explain the fact that the historian who wrote Acts definitely claims that you *did* consult with Peter and others in *public*?' and 'Could you be more precise as to the location of these churches you were writing to?' are both questions which could stump the interviewee, unless he had studied the general relation between Acts and the historical content of Galatians.

It is obvious now why the interrogator should be the better informed of the two. It is up to him to create the kind of question that will promote thought in the whole group as well as the one being interviewed, and will open the door to further study. In other words, he uses this contrived situation to expose areas of ignorance which could be made good by study, so making people desire knowledge which up to that moment they had not coveted. This, of course, is the essence of the so-called situational method of teaching, and it has great value in this kind of activity Bible study. For this method, background knowledge is only seen to be meaningful when it is actually wanted by the student.

Paul is a 'natural' for this kind of study because he commits himself so much in his writings. Someone could be put up to justify his 'boasting passages' of 2 Corinthians; his defence before Agrippa could be analysed; two members who knew Romans well could discuss what place Paul still really reserved for the Jews in his theology. The technique, however, holds good for any biblical character or writer, depending on the knowledge and interests of the group. The letters of James, Peter and John can each be discussed with their 'authors', rather as new writers are sometimes interviewed today. The Old Testament is rich in characters, but, generally speaking, a greater knowledge of the text would be required to make any discussion really meaningful. Depth interviews with Joseph, Jacob, Abraham and the like would help to recover each from the over-simplified folk-hero image that he will have become in the minds of most Christians. And as a final test, one may like to try interviewing two Isaiahs at once!

Visuals 8

There is possibly no end to the variety of answers that might result from asking a particular question of a passage of Scripture. The question is this: 'Here are words which carry a meaning for us; is there any visual way in which we can clarify and illustrate that meaning?' If the answer is yes the keen student could go on to attempt his visual commentary. He may eventually have to reject his attempt as being less powerful than the original words themselves; he may appear to waste valuable time in attempting the impossible; he may find that preoccupation with his chosen medium diverts him from his search for truth – all these dangers lie open to him, as they do in any activity method of learning. Nonetheless, there is the equal possibility of striking hidden treasure.

The possibilities are great because in principle any known form of communication of ideas can be put to the service of communicating scriptural truth. Only a sample of suggestions need be made by way of illustration.

1. Situation comedy is very much the vogue in television. What about devising a situation which enshrines Paul's teaching on family relationships as set out in Ephesians 5:22–6:9 and Colossians 3:18–4:17? There could be a rehearsed conversation between a wife, husband, child, servant and master, which indicates the advice each must follow, and presents some of the practical difficulties one meets with when trying to apply written advice. Alternatively, one could stylise the characters (in the style of modern satirical comedy) and concoct a ridiculous situation arising from the literal obeying of the advice given. A third way would be to let each character soliloquise, without dialogue with the others, in a way which illustrates how written advice can be lived out in practice.

2. Galatians 4:21–31 contains a difficult analogy with Old Testament characters. Set out the argument in diagram form, or use some form of model in which individual pieces represent first themselves, then the concept for which they stand. Visualisation is one of the best ways to understand analogies and protracted similes, in which Scripture abounds. Could the Revelation, the ultimate in imagery, be approached in this way? It is worth a try.

3. Words tend to roll off the tongue without really conjuring up for us the values they are supposed to represent. We can read horrific lists of vices (see Col. 3:5; Rom. 1:28–32) and glorious pictures of goodness (Col. 3:12; Gal. 5:22–23) without consciously thinking of such values as they reveal themselves in actual behaviour. Yet even the attempt to dramatise the conflict between the two can be a profound exercise. The actual result may be a short sequence as in a pageant, with one group expressing itself evilly then virtuously, the change coming about through the influence of Scripture as it is exhorted by a narrator. Meanwhile, however, the group may have had a searching discussion as they rejected one dramatic idea after another in their search for the right one. For example, is there any common

gesture or movement which, without words, will be recognised by all onlookers as suggesting *either* evil *or* good!

4. The dramatic approach is also useful when considering thought progressions in the Bible. Take, for instance, the progression in Romans 5:3–5 RSV 'suffering produces endurance ... character ... hope'. Was there meant to be a progression? In other words, does the right approach to life situations bring about maturity *in that order*? Well, consider and act out life situations in miniature, to find the answer. Then ask whether or not we should be looking for a similar progression in 2 Peter 1:5–7 'Supplement your faith with virtue ...' This may lead the group to look at other accumulations which might or might not contain hidden progressions. For instance, what about Psalm 1:1 RSV 'Walks ... stands ... sits', or Isaiah 40:31 RSV 'Mount up ... run ... walk'?

5. There is drama potential in any passage portraying contrast or conflict, or which employs strong word-pictures. Psalms, Isaiah, Proverbs, Job, Ecclesiastes – they all abound in such, and could therefore be approached visually. Take Psalm 107 which offers its own dramatic form as well as content. It contains three clear word-pictures in some detail: people in a lost, wilderness situation (vv. 2–7); slaves (vv. 10–16); sailors in a storm (vv. 23–30). Each physical situation is clearly analogous to a spiritual condition, and in each situation people are exhorted similarly: 'Let them thank the Lord for his enduring love and for the marvellous things he has done for men.' Such a passage could be powerfully mimed.

This kind of portrayal, it must be admitted, is probably more suitable for public presentation; moreover, it requires a group that is able and free enough to attempt co-ordinated, stylised miming. Nevertheless, it is the kind of activity which may well arise out of a creative approach to Bible study, and which produces a surprising amount of casual study discussion during rehearsal.

Though discussion seems to have come more into its own as a study technique, the debate, which is in effect a formalised discussion, is far less in favour. The very disciplines of the debate may contribute to its non-use, though it is in these that its study value lies. A debate demands the reasoned presentation of a firm argument and its counter-argument, and equally prepared supporting material for each viewpoint. This makes the participant seek for the best approach he can find, and puts his knowledge and interpretation of Scripture on the spot. In return, he is given the rare chance of developing an idea without interruption and in full, a luxury which the cut-and-thrust of discussion rarely allows.

What is perhaps off-putting about the debate as a means of Bible study is that one is not quite sure how to conclude it. The laws of debate call for a vote to be taken after the summing up by the principal speakers, with the tacit assumption that the vote will be in favour of the better presented argument, rather than of the argument which actually commends itself more to the voters. This smacks of artificiality, and people question how far one should employ a formalised method in the service of a serious study of Scripture, which by its very nature seems to carry a message which does not allow of debate anyway.

There are one or two answers to this. One is, in fact, to dispense with the voting procedure, and use the debating technique only as a suitable means of persuading members to assemble their thoughts coherently. There is nothing unethical about this, as some might imply – a method is after all only a method – and a lively debate will easily survive the absence of a count-up at the end.

The other answer is to reserve the debate for motions which do allow genuine differences of opinion anyway, even though the motion is lifted from Scripture. Now if the group leader suggests, 'This house moves that "all men have sinned and come short of the glory of God"', the debate is likely to be a non-starter in the first place. However well argued against, such a motion is bound to be defeated in any Bible study, and the convinced Christian who is asked to oppose the motion will have to force himself into the role of the devil's advocate.

Moving on through the same letter to the Romans, however, one comes across the statement, 'Every person must submit to the supreme authorities (Rom. 13:1)'. Now here is a principle of conduct which, taken at its face value, has genuine supporters and protagonists within the Christian faith itself. What is more, Scripture can be freely invoked to both support and oppose the motion! This is, therefore, a valid motion for debate in the context of study, and should lead to a clearer understanding of what this kind of text means. Moreover, taking a vote, on whatever grounds (and in practice it is difficult to keep separate one's impartial appreciation of an argument and one's personal acceptance of it) it is a natural and positive conclusion to such a debate.

Other texts which could form the basis for debating motions:

It is a good thing for a man to have nothing to do with women. (1 Cor. 7:1)
Be content with your wages. (Luke 3:14 RSV)

The choice of a debating subject is important in another way. Not only should it allow of genuine difference of approach, but it should also encourage the development of arguments with constant reference to other Scripture. In other words, speakers should be able to structure their contributions around key passages or texts of the Bible, if the exercise is to remain a Bible study in the strict sense of the word. Of course, one can rifle the Bible for debating motions which are only the spring-board for other things. 'Your meetings tend to do more harm than good' (1 Cor. 11:17), would be an ideal beginning to a debate on the quality of our modern worship! Corroborative evidence, however, would come from observation of ourselves and not from a study of Scripture, and people might go home after a profitable evening which still advanced them not at all in their understanding of the Bible. But then, this is a built-in hazard of all Bible study, of worship itself, so it is not peculiar to the debating method, or activity methods in general.

3
Line-by-Line Study

There is a form of Bible study which can be looked on as a bridge between the creative types of study so far dealt with, and the more formal, intellectualised study with which people are more familiar. It concerns itself with the meaning of words and concepts, but is still willing to play with them as literary ideas. It accepts the benefits of discussion, but uses them only in controlled situations. The leader is very much in evidence, but he has ensured wide participation before even undertaking the study.

Essentially, the method is to take a short passage of Scripture (about fifty words, summarised from a longer passage if necessary) and treat it analytically, centring study around five or six key phrases. The leader brings other relevant parts of Scripture to bear on each phrase to determine its meaning and its value to us as a devotional aid. This usually means the leader choosing the other Scripture beforehand, writing out the references (or preferably the whole quotation) and distributing them to the group.

The method has the effect of changing the subject and mood of the study every ten minutes or so. Discussion around the first phrase may call for the pooling of personal experience; the next may use collected texts in a choric format or as the basis of artificial argument or contrived dialogue; the next might call for a personal search of Scripture or hymn book; the next for intellectual consideration of a point raised by the commentators; and so on. This varied approach reduces the danger of the study deteriorating into prolonged, often undirected, discussion about familiar subjects; it also ensures that the leader has enough material to sustain the whole period.

Participation by means of prepared texts is important. The approach could be attempted without this, but the study might then soon become a one-way thing. In this context (though, as we have seen, not in all others) prior preparation by the leader is quite impressive, and the whole atmosphere of the study is healthily sharpened. As a practical point, as many as thirty to forty references may be handed round the group, so leaders should devise a clear way to make sure that the right texts are read out at the right time. For instance, if the study has been divided into six sections, each group of texts could carry serial numbers 1 to 6, or letters A to F, or the like. Having seen the use to which the first series of texts was put, later groups will wonder what their assignment is to be, but that is all to the good. It will not be long before group members are suggesting their own variants.

Such studies can be undertaken by groups up to forty strong, so are particularly suited to plenary sessions at conferences, where the numbers involved are often too great to undertake the activity-centred studies described earlier.

Not all types of Scripture will respond to the method. The need is for concentrated prose, not repeating itself unduly, and offering key phrases which allow separate treatment. These conditions exclude most narrative passages, repetitive poetry, those chapters or letters which take too long to make a point, etc. They favour such as the prayers in Paul's letters, and the majestic conclusions or purple passages of doctrinal sections. An example of each of these types is presented now in detail, as the method will be better understood when illustrated.

STUDY ONE

We pray that you may **bear fruit** in **active goodness** of every kind, and grow in **the knowledge of God**. May he strengthen you, in his glorious might, with **ample power** to meet **whatever comes** with fortitude, patience, and joy; and to give thanks to the Father who has made you fit to share

the heritage of God's people in the realm of light. (Col. 1:10–12)

All parts of this prayer are beautiful, and can obviously be studied, but the phrases in bold type have been selected in this instance.

bear fruit

This can be treated in an informal, unprepared way, starting discussion off with this kind of question:

1) How common is this particular word-picture in Scripture? Can the group remember similar references to fruit-bearing, crops, vines, seeds, growth in general, in relation to spiritual life?

2) Is this still a helpful picture for the group? Does it help to describe personal spiritual experience for them, even if they have no particular contact with, or appreciation of, nature?

3) All illustrations are said to break down somewhere. Where is this illustration deficient? In other words, at what points does natural growth cease to be an analogy for spiritual growth?

The leader can naturally prepare his own answers to these questions, drawing up cross-reference lists of texts, thinking in advance of the phrase. The average study group, however, will be quite able to supply Bible parallels, and to answer the set of questions from personal knowledge. The last question will be the most difficult to have answered, as people are not accustomed to approaching Bible imagery from a literary point of view, and therefore to looking objectively at the limitations of words and figures of speech. The exercise is worth trying if only to reassure the occasional group member who may inwardly have wondered why he had not been particularly helped through the years by this or that text.

active goodness

The aim of this exercise is to get the group to rejoice that people do still practise goodness today, or, in other words, that fruit is still being borne in individual lives. The exercise has the important secondary aim of persuading people to pay a tribute to, give witness on behalf of, someone else, without embarrassment, in the natural context of group study.

The group should be invited to listen to a sequence of quotations taken from those passages of Paul's letters which contain his personal greetings and recommendations. The quotations, before being distributed, should be slightly altered so as to contain no individual's name. This will help the group to think less specifically about the references, in order to answer the question, 'Does this description fit anybody *you* know? If so, tell us about him or her.' Here are samples of such references:

He is our dear brother and trustworthy helper in the Lord's work. I am sending him to you on purpose ... to **put fresh heart into you.** (Eph. 6:21–22)
(Question to ask: 'Do you know anyone who usually manages to put fresh heart, hope, into you, by his presence, words, example, etc.?)
You should honour men like him; in Christ's cause he came near to death, **risking his life to render me the service.** (Phil. 2:30)
I can vouch for him, that **he works tirelessly for you** and the people. (Col. 4:13)
Going to the limit of their resources ... they begged us ... to be allowed to share in this generous service ... And their giving surpassed our expectations. (2 Cor. 8:3).
Give her ... a welcome worthy of God's people, and stand by her in any business in which she may need your help, for **she has herself been a good friend to many, including myself.** (Romans 16:2)

The average group will probably offer some striking parallels, after careful priming, and this kind of exercise can often be repeated in different forms. It will have the effect of making members appreciative of the truth that the Spirit of God still reveals himself in the ordinary actions of faithful men and women.

the knowledge of God

It is often helpful to face up to the contradictions of Scripture, those many occasions on which the Bible uses the same words in conflicting ways (see chapter 6 for fuller treatment of this matter). The word 'knowledge' is one example, for one could well ask what it is that we can hope to *know* about God, if Scripture is true. Do we all have knowledge? What kind of knowledge is it – understanding, wisdom, intimacy, information? Could any member of the group offer a definition of spiritual knowledge, such as Paul is referring to in this prayer, as a discussion starter?

The discussion can be approached by distributing in advance a sequence of texts which superficially contradict each other. The text readers are asked to develop an argument amongst themselves, each sticking faithfully to his text. One brave soul starts the ball rolling, followed, perhaps, by someone whose text says the opposite. He in turn is supported or gainsaid by someone else, and so on. Each reader can repeat his text as often as he wishes, or repeat only significant phrases from it, for effect. If a real argumentative spirit can be acted out within the group, so much the better.

This is the kind of text to put forward:

All that may be known of God by men lies plain before their eyes. (Romans 1:19)
He dwells in unapproachable light. No man has ever seen or ever can see him. (1 Tim. 6:16)
I know who it is in whom I have trusted. (2 Tim. 1:12)
Can you fathom the mystery of God, can you fathom the perfection of the Almighty? (Job. 11:7)
Jesus said, 'I have disclosed to you everything that I heard from my Father.' (John 15:15)
How unsearchable [God's] judgements, how untraceable his ways! Who knows the mind of the Lord? (Rom. 11:33)
He has made known to us his hidden purpose – such was his will and pleasure. (Eph. 1:9)

He has given men a sense of time past and future, but no comprehension of God's work from beginning to end. (Eccles. 3:11)
The Lord God does nothing without giving to his servants ... knowledge of his plans. (Amos 3:7).

As already explained, the next thing to do is to ask someone to attempt a brief reconciliation of these texts. His statement can be altered or polished by the whole group, until people are in basic agreement with what they might expect to be included in their 'knowledge of God'.

ample power

This phrase is only representative of the earlier part of that sentence, which is a typical accumulation of superlatives, some of them grammatically superfluous: 'strengthen ... glorious might ... ample power ... whatever comes'. We are at least left in no doubt as to the adequacy of God's energy! Nonetheless, this is a common literary ploy of biblical writers, and it may prove helpful to let the group loose on Scripture (or a hymn book) to collect, and to exult in, other examples of the same feature. People will soon light on 'exceeding abundantly above all', 'overwhelming victory', 'breadth and length and depth and height', etc. Someone else may light on the Hebrew poets' trick of repetition for effect, in evidence so much in the Psalms. The thing is that once people are persuaded to go searching Scripture on their own, they come up with their own gems for the building up of all, and are continually strengthening their own grasp of the total lay-out of the Bible.

whatever comes

A phrase such as this allows the group to realise its function a little more deeply. To begin with, it may be desirable to look at the phrase a little light-heartedly. Assume, for instance, that 'whatever comes' is interpreted pessimistically. Disheartening phrases can be plucked from the Bible (not all of them in strict context), and the group members receiving these phrases in the distribution of texts can be asked to form themselves into an impromptu choric group, experimenting with the words to form some kind of doleful chant (remember those witches on the blasted heath in amateur *Macbeth*!), e.g., whoever had 'Groans' to say from the list given below can actually groan on and on, rather than say the actual word! The effect will be crude, possibly chaotic, probably hilarious, but certainly justified, if followed up properly. The kind of phrases which would make up the script would include:

WARS!	RUMOURS OF WARS!	PLAGUES!
GROANS!	VANITY AND VEXATION!	FAMINES!
NO HOPE!	FRUSTRATION!	NO GOD!

This facile exercise is only preparatory to asking group members to talk about what they personally fear most about their own future, 'whatever comes'. We may not have the pessimistic view of life which such a dismal catalogue conjures up, but we certainly have particular fears. People may be afraid that some hitherto untried experience of life may threaten and collapse their faith, and they may be willing to talk about such fears. If they do so, the study is being used to work one of its profoundest works – allowing Christians to share their understandable anxieties about matters of faith, in the context of the Scripture which is the ground of their faith.

the heritage of God's people

This huge phrase can be treated at two or three levels, depending on the interests and capacity of the group.

1) The phrase can be taken to mean the advantages and strengths of God's people as a community. What, then, are those strengths? Can the group spell out the practical and spiritual benefits of the faith that they share?

2) The phrase can be given its more normal individualistic interpretation, as if each Christian receives his inheritance in terms of what happens in himself as a person. In other words,

what kind of person, in terms of character and principle, will a man be when he lives as an heir of God?

3) More ambitiously, one can take the idea of heritage further. Even the individual of any generation is, in some sense, heir to all the faith and works that have accumulated through all the preceding generations. This gives his heritage a cosmic significance, making it much bigger, more mystical than perhaps he has thought. The group may care to come to grips with this concept. If there is any reluctance to do so, on the grounds that the idea is far-fetched and irrelevant, the class could be presented with texts such as the following, and asked what they are trying to say:

> The created universe waits with eager expectation for God's sons to be revealed. (Rom. 8:19)
> It is God's hidden purpose ... that the universe ... might be brought into a unity in Christ. (Eph. 1:10)
> He annulled the law ... so as to create ... a single new humanity ... You too are being built ... into a spiritual dwelling for God. (Eph. 2:15, 22)
> In this final age he has spoken to us in the Son whom he has made heir to the whole universe. (Heb. 1:2)

Leaders may well reject this third alternative, because the questions which the texts raise are too philosophical, or outside the scope of the kind of person who attends devotional studies. It would be unfortunate if this decision were made every time the possibility occurred. Bible studies, even of the devotional type, should not simply be confirming what the group already knows about the Bible or about itself. This is too often all that happens. The group should also be challenged to come to grips with new or forgotten concepts which lie scarcely hidden in Scripture, but which the eye or the mind has learnt to glide over and ignore. One may refer to the chapter on true-to-life studies for further development of this thought.

'He has **forgiven** us **all our sins**; he has cancelled **the bond** which pledged us to the decrees of the law. It stood against us, but he has set it aside, **nailing it to the cross.** On that cross he discarded the **cosmic powers and authorities like a garment.**' (Col. 2:13–15)

He has forgiven us

This phrase immediately strikes a personal note, perhaps more personal than the group wishes to hear, and a semi-objective approach may help. Making sure first that each member has his own pencil and paper, a variety of texts is read out, all of which say essentially, 'God has forgiven me.' The point is that as varied and literary a selection as possible should be read out, giving each individual the chance to say to himself, 'Does this description fit *my* experience of forgiveness? Would I have thought of my experience in those terms?' With ample time for reflection between each text, each member can then make his own selection of Scripture to describe his own case. The pencil and paper will let him keep his own table of ticks and crosses, hits and misses, as a basis for later discussion.

Each leader will have his own favourite expressions; here is a sample group from Psalms:

He reached down from the height and took me, he drew me me out of mighty waters. (18:16)
He makes me lie down in green pastures, and leads me beside the waters of peace. (23:2)
Unfailing love enfolds him who trusts in the Lord. (32:10)
He brought me up out of the mire and clay; he set my feet on a rock. (40:2)
From far away you understand all my thoughts. (139:2 GNB)

A dozen such poetic descriptions would be an adequate selection, and the leader should not hesitate to include word-pictures which seem to him archaic or irrelevant. It is astonishing how the individual circumstances of modern lives are exactly described by poetic fancies. The texts chosen should allow the group to be answering such questions as: 'Did you find the majority/minority of these descriptions helpful? Do we need this kind of language? If not, is it because we are not as a race given to such poetic expressions, or because our own gratitude for forgiveness is not strong enough to warrant them? Does any description *exactly* fit, because of a particular personal experience? What has the exercise told you about biblical language in general?'

There should be no lack of comment after this exercise, and the leader should aim to extract it. On the other hand, he will *not* look for uninhibited discussion after the next phase of study.

all our sins

Members now read to each other biblical descriptions both of particular evils and of basically wrong attitudes to life. Again, the group is asked to record, quite privately, its reactions to the list. The question to be answered *on paper* is: 'Have you at any time committed any of these sins, or been aware of answering the basic descriptions given?' Here is a suggested list of references (in some cases the tense of the original has been altered to allow listeners to identify themselves more easily with it):

You were heading for destruction, appetite was your God, and you gloried in your shame. (Phil. 3:19)
Your minds were set on earthly things. (Phil. 3:19)
You obeyed the commander of the spiritual powers of the air. (Eph. 2:2)
You lived your lives in sensuality, and obeyed the promptings of your own instincts and notions. (Eph. 2:3)
Your world was a world without hope and without God. (Eph. 2:12)
You were God's enemies in heart and mind, and your deeds were evil. (Col. 1:21)
Fornication . . . indecency . . . lust . . . ruthless greed. (Col. 3:5)

Anger ... passion ... malice ... cursing ... filthy talk.
(Col. 3:8)

The questions to ask now are: 'Are these descriptions any more
useful than those concerning forgiveness? If you reject the general
descriptions (most will), is this because the language is extrava-
gant, or because you did not have this problem or attitude in the
first place? What does this tell us about ourselves, and about the
people Paul wrote to? Are they any different from us?' It will
also be useful to know whether there were any descriptions with
which the whole group agreed or disagreed.

All these questions should evoke useful discussion. The
question *not* to ask is, 'Which of these sins did you have to put a
tick against?' People in study groups must be reassured that at all
times their privacy is safeguarded, even before they are asked to
examine themselves. Otherwise, a devotional study would become an inquisition which people are unlikely to attend again
voluntarily. The point is that, whether they speak about it or
not, people, by silent reflection, are brought to see themselves in
the light of Scripture. If they then wish to share a reflection with
the whole group, they will do so unbidden, and that is real sharing.

the bond

It will be as well for the leader to consult commentaries on this
point, to be in a position to give pointers as to the meaning of
this part of the text. The word-picture seems to have been used
basically to stress that the weight of wrongdoing and wrong
thinking for which we need forgiveness is there *by our own
admission*, and not just because God has unilaterally said we are
guilty. The Law demanded a standard; we did not keep the
standard; and the bond or confession acknowledging the difference is in our own handwriting.

We can therefore enlist the word, as used in this context, to
allow the group to look for its own descriptions; statements
with which individuals are happy to identify themselves, because

48

they went in personal search of them. For instance, members can be encouraged to look into their hymn book to see how other post-biblical Christians have confessed their guilt. A glance into some of the acknowledged great hymns would unearth confessions such as:

False and full of sin I am.

I need Thy presence every passing hour;
What but Thy grace can foil the tempter's power?

Frail children of dust and feeble as frail.

My richest gain I count but loss,
And pour contempt on all my pride.

Naked, come to Thee for dress,
Helpless, look to Thee for grace,
Foul, I to the fountain fly.

It may be that the occasional group member has worked out his own situation in writing, having written a poem or song, or in some other way attempted to express himself. This kind of probing study often unearths such treasures. However, the group is more likely to be content to delve into other people's writings to find words that they wish they had written.

nailing it to the cross

Here again recourse to the commentaries will help. (It could even be a separate activity for members to read out short, prepared extracts from three or four different commentaries). Certainly, Paul is using his imagination in implying that our self-written voluntary confession is taken by Christ and nailed to the cross as the reason for his crucifixion, in accordance with the then prevailing custom that each cross should carry a written explanation of why the victim was being punished. The group can carry this imagination one step further by surmising: 'Had

Christ actually been allowed to write his own superscription, and had decided to use words he had previously used in talking to the people, what kind of words do we think he would have used?' Having understood that this was frankly an exercise of the imagination, the group will not be slow in thinking of some of the great claims of Christ on our behalf:

I have come into this world ... to give sight to the sightless and to make blind those who see. (John 9:39)
I have come that men may have life, and may have it in all its fullness. (John 10:10)
I lay down my life for the sheep. (John 10:15)
I have not come to judge the world, but to save the world. (John 12:47)
God has sent me to announce good news to the poor ... to let the broken victims go free. (Luke 4:18)

Such texts could be previously distributed, but read out *after* members have put forward their own suggestions.

cosmic powers and authorities

If necessary, many references could be added to this one to show that, for the New Testament writer, the supernatural world was real and impinged on the 'natural' world for both good and ill. At this point in the study, therefore, a period of free discussion on the subject would be appropriate.

Sample feeder questions would be: What are we to make of such references in Scripture? Do they illustrate simply one way of speaking about aspects of life which we now describe differently? Have you had any experience in life which you are obliged to explain in terms of coming into contact with 'cosmic powers and authorities'? If not, do you accept the validity of supernatural experiences for others (spirits, visitations, etc.)? If you are sceptical, does such biblical language as this lessen the book's authenticity for you; and how do you account for the whole phenomenon of the 'Holy Ghost'? What do you really believe about Satan, angels, spirits? What is the biblical teaching about this area of belief? What has the Church taught, and why?

like a garment

It is no evasion of a problem to conclude this study with the thought that, whatever the exact nature and strength of the forces levelled against the Christian, Christ's strength is proof against them. The difference between them is vividly shown in the simple illustration that Christ discards opposition as easily as if he were taking off a coat! It is the measure of this triumph which this study dwells on now. This can be done in one or two ways:

1) By presenting a number of texts showing how comprehensively Christ dealt with opposition when on earth in the flesh.

2) By quoting from other definitive statements in Scripture which give the final victory to Christ.

3) By inviting personal experience and witness to Christ's triumph in individual lives.

It is hoped that these extended notes on two studies may show the versatility and potential of this method. One more general point may be made. Care has been taken to suggest the kind of question which one may ask when trying to take the class from activity to discussion. The leader should give careful thought to his choice of question, because the wrong questions can make much discussion still-born. If the question is too broad the result is too often vague generalisations ('Well, it all depends . . .' is frequently the sign of sterile to-and-fro discussion to come) and huge conclusions which no one in the group, even the leader, is competent enough to summarise and present in a fruitful way that might lead to action. If the question is too personal, people will get afraid or resentful, not wishing to trust their revelation or real opinion to the judgment of the group. If the question asks only for a statement of fact, then only those people can answer it who happen to know the fact. And so on. On the other hand, good questions will lead to good answers, and follow-up of the kind of exercise described above will depend largely on whether the leader can ask the kind of question which will win the trust and response of the group.

In closing, here are some other passages which could be suitably studied in this way (in each instance the passages are a précis):

I have learned to find **resources in myself whatever the circumstances.** I have been very thoroughly initiated into **the human lot** with all its ups and downs – **fullness and hunger, plenty and want.** I have strength for anything through **him who gives me power** (Phil. 4:11–14)

In **our natural condition** we lay under **the dreadful judgement of God.** But God, **rich in mercy,** brought us to **life with Christ,** so that he might display in **the ages to come** how immense are **the resources of his grace.** For we are **God's handiwork.** (Eph. 2:3–10)

For the word of God is **alive and active.** It cuts more keenly than **any two-edged sword,** piercing as far as **the place where life and spirit,** joints and marrow, **divide.** It sifts **the purposes and thoughts** of the heart. Everything lies exposed to the eyes of **the One with whom we have to reckon.** (Heb. 4:12–13)

4
Quizzes

11

One can argue strongly that what we know as a Bible quiz has little real place in a mature study group, except as an interest raiser, or as light relief. Quizzes are techniques for testing knowledge possessed, rarely for accumulating new knowledge. Moreover, the knowledge tested by quizzes is usually factual. 'Who was Isaac's father?' has only one answer (if there is only one Isaac!) and one must already know the fact before giving the answer.

Furthermore, it is questionable whether many of the facts unearthed by quizzes are worth remembering in any case. Do students of the word of God in its most basic sense really need to know the names of three trees mentioned in the Bible, the meaning of the actual word 'Gethsemane', the names of Noah's sons, any five of the plagues, etc. The point is debatable. We should perhaps distinguish between the various kinds of biblical knowledge so that we can recognise which kind we would do better to seek after.

1) There is the apprehension of God's dealings with man and men as shown in the Bible. To learn this, we must be distilling from the wealth of words those divine truths which undergird human history and behaviour. This kind of knowledge is the outstanding goal of serious study groups.

2) There is a working knowledge of the Bible itself which helps a student to get at that distilled truth. Knowing the general layout of Scripture, its broad divisions, the places where particular truths are spelt out most clearly, the textual norms for teaching, perhaps detailed memory knowledge of key passages – this is necessary factual knowledge, tools for the search, all too often lacking in the modern Christian.

3) There is the wealth of detail such as was hinted at above, of undoubted interest to a Bible lover, but not furthering at all the search for eternal truth. That search may in fact be hindered, if people substitute this bibliolatrous approach for true study. There is a danger of treating the accumulation of biblical bric-à-brac as a hobby, coming to the book as to a set book in literature, treasuring its humanness and not its mysteries. Harmless, even praiseworthy – until it puts others off the trail by its cosy inconsequence.

The question to be asked in this chapter, therefore, is: can the quiz technique be used to lead the group into essential scriptural knowledge? The answer will be 'Yes', provided the means used is seen only as a gateway, and the group remains aware of its ultimate goal.

INTERPRETATIVE QUIZZES

Here is a series of quizzes which have similar aims:
1) to test the group's ability to place biblical statements in their context.
2) to illustrate the extent to which Scripture has found its way into literature and life.
3) to highlight the variety of interpretations which individual texts can undergo.
4) to develop the group's own ability to think about the essential meaning of Scripture, and express its thoughts clearly.

These ambitions illustrate the previous point that the quiz aspect is really incidental, as only the first of these aims can be factually expressed and measured. If leaders wish to assign actual marks to answers, it would have to be some kind of impression marking judging how well the quizzee has thought through the question and worded his answer.

Literary Quotes

Here is a list of quotations from famous writers and poets. Each passage contains a clear reference to Scripture, and offers a personal reflection on it. The quiz is: (a) to identify the original Scripture, placing it in its context (who said it, to whom, in what situation, where found in the Bible); (b) to express in plain words what this writer seemed to be saying with the help of that Scripture.

For I am tolerant, generous, keep no rules,
    And the age honours me.
Thank God, I am not as these rigid fools,
    Even as this Pharisee.   Alice Meynell (ref. Luke 18:11)

Weary and mud-bespattered, but quite possessed of his ordinary clearness of brain, he sat down by the well, thinking as he did so what a poor Christ he made.   Thomas Hardy (John 4:6)

Once at least in his life each man walks with Christ to Emmaus. Oscar Wilde (Luke 24:13)

By such small beginnings – a smile, a shot, a single sentence such as 'Follow me' – is a man's path determined; and sometimes we are lucky not to know it.   Nicholas Monsarrat (Matt. 4:19)

Now he saw clearly whence came all the horrors he had seen, and what ought to be done to put an end to them. The answer he had been unable to find was the same that Christ gave to Peter. It was to forgive always, every one, to forgive an infinite number of times, because there are none who are not themselves guilty, and therefore none who can punish or reform.   Leo Tolstoy (Matt. 18:22)

The worst of those Eastern fakirs hung on hooks is that they are too conspicuous. It may make them just a little vain. I don't deny that Stylites and some of the first hermits may have been touched with the same danger. But our friend Marillac is a Christian anchorite; and understands the advice, 'When you fast, anoint your head and wash your face'. He is not seen of men to fast. On the contrary, he is seen of men to feast. Only, don't you see, he has invented a new kind of fasting. G. K. Chesterton (Matt. 6:17)

They sit at the Feet – they hear the Word – they see how truly the Promise runs.
They have cast their burden upon the Lord, and – the Lord He lays it on Martha's Sons!   Rudyard Kipling (Luke 10:42)

Note that these quotes are taken from writers who were not writing religious books at the time. This fact could hold special interest for the class. One could compile an equally attractive list of quotes from devotional books, commentaries, etc. The writers of such, however, tend to be more direct in their interpretation, rather than allusive. They say what they think the text means, so leave less to the imagination of the group.

It is not necessary to leave the answering of a question to one individual every time unless the element of competition is introduced. The group as a whole can be asked to improve on, or differ from, an individual's first attempt, so moving into true study discussion.

Headlines, posters, book titles

Much can be gained from keeping one's eyes open for the occasions when a text or biblical phrase is pressed into service by the secular media. The reference may appear casual, but it presupposes that the reader will recognise and follow the allusion, and we can easily be led into profitable debate by analysing the use to which it is put. For example:

Headlines. These headlines appeared recently:

'This vengeance is mine' (statement by a father after the murder of his daughter)
Eat, drink and be merry – if you dare! (following a Budget speech)

Advertising occasionally has recourse to Scripture:

Make Hovis *your* daily bread.
A Child in the Midst (Shaftesbury Society)

Book titles often use this ploy, and reading the book will frequently reveal powerful and original applications of the phrase. The leader can introduce the study with a précis of the book itself, or perhaps ask one of the group to review it for him. An imaginative group could be asked to devise its own story around the phrase, so as to throw a new light on the text. Some actual titles observed are:

Some trust in Chariots
Pipers in the Market-Place
My Son, My Son
The Blood of the Lamb
No Need of the Sun

The recommended sequence for study in all these cases, to make the exercise profitable, is:

1) Identify the original quotation, so placing all biblical knowledge in context.
2) Be satisfied as to its original meaning.
3) Consider the particular use to which the quote has been put.
4) Evaluate any new light thus thrown upon Scripture.

Figures of speech

Much discussion could take place, of the kind outlined above, from a simple quizzing and scrutiny of the many figures of speech which have found their way into normal usage from the Bible. In this category one will also have to discuss any debased or reduced meanings of texts which have come about through long use in everyday speech over the years. Perhaps the class can detect some particular direction in which phrases tend to lose their original meaning. Is there also a pattern in the *kind* of text which has become popular?

Examples:
   To kill the fatted calf.
   Be sure your sin will find you out.
   It covers a multitude of sins.
   Ah! the prodigal returns.
   Hiding your light under a bushel.
   The mark of Cain.
   Salt of the earth.
   In the lion's den.
   Eat, drink and be merry.
   Weary in well-doing.

The Bible and hymns

   Hymns are an important and lucrative source of quiz material. There are very few hymns or spiritual songs which do not make reference to specific Scripture, or indeed are not indebted to the Bible for their basic thoughts and meaning. The more a congregation relies on the singing of hymns as an integral part of worship, the more it should consider the words and worth of those songs. In a real sense, people sing Scripture when they sing hymns. Sometimes, as with the hymns of Charles Wesley, they sing what amounts to a mosaic of Scripture, built up of fragments from all parts of the Bible, yet put to personal and distinctive use. At other times, the hymns are frank paraphrases of passages of Scripture such as the Psalms. Because hymns hold such a special place in the lives of worshippers, they offer an attractive approach to the study of the Bible. Here are some suggestions:

Hymn analysis. Simply take a favourite hymn and try, as a group, to trace its language and thought back into the Bible. This means, for instance, looking for clear, unambiguous quotations from Scripture. When James Montgomery began his hymn, 'For ever with the Lord', he was obviously remembering that Paul had written, 'So shall we be for ever with the Lord' (1 Thess. 4:17 AV). 'Abide with me, fast falls the eventide', is an echo of 'Abide with us: for it is towards evening' (Luke 24:29AV). And so on.

The pool of study is virtually endless, at least almost as large as the congregation's hymnbook itself.

As well as seeking to simply identify the origin of the expressions, the group can be asking itself, What variety of sources does this song draw upon, how many different biblical books, from Old and New Testaments? Does a poet have favourite sources? (The group could study a selection of one hymn writer's pieces in one sitting to decide this.) Is the scriptural sense changed in any way by the use of it in the hymn? Is the use forced, natural, valid, effective, helpful, enlightening, confusing?

Given some experience in this kind of exercise, it can be taken in reverse, though with rather more difficulty. Take a Bible verse, preferably a well-known promise or doctrinal statement, and try to trace its use through hymnody in general, working from memory or whatever study aid may be available. Again, one may ask whether the use of the chosen text is always consistent? Are there any interesting variants of it? Done often enough, this kind of exercise eventually feeds directly back into worship, as people's awareness of the value of hymns is heightened, and they will look for scriptural roots more and more naturally and successfully.

Note that when undertaking this kind of study, the group should use the King James Version, being the one which is almost exclusively quoted by hymn writers (although, to be thorough, one should also have on hand the Prayer Book Version of the Psalms, much used, for instance, by Charles Wesley). Suitable texts to trace through hymns would include Matt. 11:28, 1 John 1:7-9, John 3:16, Psalm 51:7, Psalm 23, Rev. 22:1.

Word origins. There are many hymn allusions which cannot be traced back to a single text, but are obviously scriptural for all that. This is because the words are used over and over again in the Bible, and therefore in hymns, though they have little currency elsewhere. In this case, the task of the quiz would be to establish the general scriptural use of the word, then discuss its use in hymns much as in the previous exercise. Examples of such biblical words are: refuge, shepherd, fold, peace, praise, blessing, fountain, contrite, fullness.

Hymn roots. This is a variant of hymn analysis, but with more of a quiz approach. Several hymns, such as the two mentioned earlier, have their first lines rooted in Scripture. Give the group the text, and ask for the appropriate hymn. When this is being done satisfactorily, reverse the procedure, giving the first lines of hymns and asking the group for the *exact* Bible references on which those lines are based. Progress will be rather slower this time. Examples:

Text	*Hymn*
Neh. 9:5	Stand up and bless the Lord
Eccles. 11:6	Sow in the morn thy seed
Matt. 5:8	Blest are the pure in heart
Rev. 4:8	Holy, holy, holy, Lord God Almighty
Isa. 53:3	Man of sorrows! What a name
2 Cor. 8:9	Thou who wast rich beyond all splendour
1 Sam. 3:9	Master, speak! Thy servant heareth
Mal. 3:17	When he cometh ... to make up his jewels.

Psalm paraphrases. Here again, the exercise is to relate hymn to Scripture. The question to be asked is: Which psalms, or sections of psalms, are paraphrased by the following hymns?

Hymn	*Psalm*
The Lord's my shepherd.	23
The King of love my Shepherd is.	23
All people that on earth do dwell.	100
Praise, my soul, the King of Heaven.	103

| Through all the changing scenes of life. | 34 |

| Glorious things of thee are spoken,
Zion, city of our God. | 137 |

| O clap your hands together
All you people of the Lord. | 47 |

| Let us, with a gladsome mind,
Praise the Lord, for He is kind. | 136 |

Certain study approaches can follow: Do the hymns add to the original meaning in any way? (For example, 'The King of love' has clearly added the New Testament picture of the shepherd going after the lost sheep, whereas 'The Lord's my shepherd' is a strict paraphrase.) Or is Scripture weakened in any way? Have the Psalms been 'Christianised' in their paraphrasing? Are these particular Psalms, of which we have famous paraphrases, still valid for modern Christians? If so, are all Psalms therefore valid?

Identification quizzes. The aim of these is simply to continue indicating the hymn-Scripture link, and strengthen the group's geographical familiarity with the Bible.

1) In which biblical books will we find the original reference to the characters named in the following hymn quotations:

Love climbed the ladder Jacob saw.

Joshua fought the battle of Jericho.

Could we but climb where Moses stood.

... the grave where Lazarus slept.

What from Eli's sense was sealed
The Lord to Hannah's son revealed.

(Note that here only a few examples are given for each suggestion. Leaders will find other examples in the hymn books of their choice, and other types of questions. The principle will be the same throughout.)

2) the following hymn quotes are paraphrases of words originally spoken by Bible characters. In each case name the person who originally said it; the context in which it was said; and the *exact* original quotation, giving the source if possible.

I know that my Redeemer lives.

Almost persuaded now to believe.

Tell out, my soul, the greatness of the Lord.

Wrestling, I will not let Thee go.

Once I was blind, but now I see.

Master, speak! Thy servant heareth.

Wash me, but not my feet alone.

3) Which incidents in the life of Jesus are referred to in the following lines:

At even, when the sun was set

Who walkedst on the foaming deep,
    And calm amid its rage didst sleep.

Hark! all the tribes hosanna cry.

That kind, upbraiding glance which broke
    Unfaithful Peter's heart.

Fasting alone in the desert

Lord, be it mine like them to choose
    The better part.

4) Which parables of Jesus are being referred to in the following lines:

Give his angels charge at last
    In the fire the tares to cast.

I've found the pearl of greatest price.

The Bridegroom comes, arise!

Who trusts in God's unchanging love
    Builds on the rock which naught can move.

Sinner, we are sent to bid you
    To the gospel feast today.

5) Which Old Testament incidents are being referred to in the
following lines:

Hushed was the evening hymn,
    The temple courts were dark.

Move on the water's face.

Speak through the earthquake, wind and fire,
    O still, small voice of calm.

As noiseless let thy blessing fall
    As fell Thy manna down.

So to the Jews old Canaan stood,
    While Jordan rolled between.

6) From which biblical book do the following descriptions of
Christ originate:

O Dayspring, rise upon our night.

The lily of the valley

Sun of Righteousness, arise.

Hail, Thou Heaven-born Prince of Peace.

Jesus, our Immanuel

My Christ is Sharon's rose.

O Lamb of God, Thou wonderful Sin-bearer

Note again that even in this kind of group activity, the leader need not, should not, be content with one word half-answers. Most people will be able to offer some clue to the answer, but much fewer will give a coherent reply. Much scriptural knowledge is only half known, whereas a Bible study seeks to make it really known. So, if necessary, the group should be taken back to the original incident, or parable, or the like, to really grasp the meaning and power of the original. In other words, to be effective study wise, the quizzes should be only starting-points into research which will help the class to articulate its ideas, strengthen its memory of Scripture and understand Bible imagery and incident.

Interpretation exercises. These are similar to identification quizzes, but make the study element more explicit, and call for more effort on the part of those quizzed to explain their opinions in clear terms, and for prolonged follow-up by the whole group. Full treatment of any *one* of the sub-questions has been known to occupy an entire evening's study, with the right kind of probing group.

1) Explain, as a basis for fuller discussion, the Old Testament allusions in the following, and the use to which the hymn writer has put the allusion:

Out of my stony griefs
    Bethel I'll raise.

Solid joys and lasting treasure
    None but Zion's children know.

We see the Lord . . .
    He is high and lifted up, and his
    train fills the temple.

Enter into Thy promised rest,
    The Canaan of Thy perfect love.

Till from Mount Pisgah's lofty height
    I view my home . . .

2) Which miracles of Christ are referred to here, and how are they given a personal spiritual application by the hymn writer:

Break Thou the bread of life,
    O Lord, to me.

Reclothe us in our rightful mind.

We touch Him in life's throng and press,
    And we are whole again.

The billows that filled my poor soul with alarm
    Are hushed at His word into stillness and calm.

In childlike faith now I stretch forth my hand.

Launch out into the deep,
    And let the shoreline go!

3) With which Old Testament characters do we associate the following objects mentioned in hymns? Say something about the original purpose of the object lesson, and the use to which it is put in these hymns:

Thou art the Potter, I am the clay.

Let the fiery, cloudy pillar
    Lead me all my journey through.

I tried the broken cisterns, Lord.

Stricken rock, with streaming side.

Saw ye not the cloud arise,
    Little as a human hand?

There let my way appear
    Steps unto heaven.

Touch my lips with a coal from Thine altar, Lord.

This chapter has considered only one specialist area of the whole field of quizzes, and only a part of that restricted area. Quizzes themselves are only one of many kinds of teaching aids that are already in print to help the leader of Bible studies. It would therefore be easy to show that there is a wealth of material around for the taking. The important thing is that, in order to attract and hold serious study groups, the material must be used in a mature way, and must go far beyond the mere accumulation of oddments of knowledge about the Bible. All aids, whether in themselves or in the use the leader makes of them, must have as their target a consideration of the essential message of Scripture. After all, this message, we believe, is our strongest interest factor, our biggest selling-point.

5

Study through Subjects

Students of homiletics will know that their discipline is largely aimed at recognising and applying the various methods by which a given passage of Scripture can be expounded to a congregation. On the one hand stands the Bible itself, a piece of lively literature, perhaps not even intended to be preached upon, unregimented and multi-coloured in its content, form, structure, etc. On the other hand stands the student, holding in his mind his array of methods, his tools for prising open this oyster, faceting this jewel. From these he must select that one which will serve him best. If he selects the wrong one, he will at best be delayed in his task, at worst damage his material and perhaps never accomplish his intention. In this respect he behaves like a workman with the wrong set of wrenches, a housewife who takes up the wrong cutting tool to deal with her kitchen chore, the painter with the wrong brush. So many lifeless, malformed sermons can be traced directly to the wrong method (so right in other contexts) being forced on to the sensitive beauty of the original.

This chapter tries to describe one such tool for wresting the truth from Scripture, in the context of group study. It is a tool both valuable and dangerous, as will be seen. In essence it is simple. It is to take a passage of Scripture, and to look at it, in it, through it, from only *one* clear, restricted point of view. For the purposes of this kind of study, nothing else matters but this particular search and anything which might advance it, and the attention of the group must be drawn back to this purpose again and again. It is like the search for the goodly pearl – all other pearls must be sacrificed in order to win it.

Such a discipline is both necessary and justified in the context of study. One of the great perils of Bible studies is that people spread their thoughts too wide, are too easily sidetracked into well-trodden cul-de-sacs. The result is a net full of generally useful statements, temporary insights, half-thought ideas, and the like, with very little that is really worth keeping. It is difficult, of course, to persuade adults that this is so, for we all like to feel that *our* contributions are controlled, pertinent, stimulating. This is sadly not so, and most of us would benefit from having our minds pressed more firmly to the grindstone of directed study. At least on occasions, we have to be big enough to jettison any idea which does not directly help along the main purpose of the study, to apply standards to our words and thoughts which we would not normally demand of ourselves. In other words, in the occasional class it would be enormously beneficial to toil all night and catch - just a little!

The great danger of such an approach is that of all special-isations it can blind itself to too much. There is an allegorical story of the young boy who scrutinised the whole splendour of the Lord Mayor's Show looking exclusively for the horse's headgear that *he* had polished. A feast missed by looking for a crumb! That is the precise problem of studying the fullness of Scripture through the peep-hole of a single theme, and the leader, at least, should be aware of the delicacy of the tool he is hand-ling. It will not happen often, but he must set it aside, if need be. He is right to stop group members wandering over the same old arguments and counter-arguments; but he is wrong when he does not realise that one particular member has begun to put an age-old question from the *heart*, under the stimulus of pressing, personal need. He is also wrong to haul his group back to its task if, in its wanderings, the group has somehow stumbled into its most meaningful sharing period for months. On such occasions he must lay aside his chosen subject gladly, content to feel that the discipline he initially imposed had somehow brought about a different kind of reality.

Now to the subjects themselves. They are of quite different

types, and have therefore been classified into groups. Unsatisfactory grouping, to be sure, as one really cannot say where the intellect gives way to the spirit, where creativity begins to be secular rather than religious. At any rate, the subjects have been labelled intellectual, devotional and creative only to indicate the initial emphasis of the approach.

To avoid needless repetition, let it be repeated just this once how the method works in practice. The leader would do well to introduce the study in these words: 'We are all going to read together our study passage. While we read, and afterwards, we are going to be looking carefully for any reference, or information, or allusion in the passage which will help us to answer this *one* question . . . (insert the subject here). We have no other purpose, and we should try to give all our attention to this single problem, in the belief that the whole passage will mean more to us as a result.' In most of the examples given below the class as a whole could be helpfully subdivided into groups of three or four people, which could thrash out the assignment before sharing their findings. This is especially useful if the class decides to take a lengthy passage for study, as each sub-group could take a section of the whole as its particular province.

Intellectual Subjects   12

These will be the approaches least familiar to most groups, so will be described first in greater detail to illustrate the method.

1. Take a letter of Paul, and ask the group to scour it for all the information it contains concerning the historical background of the letter. All helpful references should be listed, those which give non-ambiguous information, those which could possibly have a bearing. The members should be encouraged to exercise imagination and stretch references to their utmost interpretation, as later group discussion will soon put the more fanciful theories out of court! In fact, the group as a whole will come to see how scholars evolve their theories relating to background,

authorship, etc. (Some will be stimulated to find out what other source material is available to help such theories to be matured.)

If a sub-group were to make discussion notes on, say, the letter to the Colossians, they might start off something like this:

1:1	'God's people at Colossae'	— here the destination is clearly named.
1:6	'the whole world over'	— letter written in time of general expansion.
1:7	'taught by Epaphras'	— Epaphras the first to evangelise Colossae? Who was he?
1:21	'estranged from God'	— could this mean that Paul was writing mainly to Gentiles?

As hinted earlier, the total harvest for the evening may appear frugal (depending on the passage for study) but it will be worth gleaning if it assures ordinary people that they have as much access to a knowledge of background history as anyone else. Such knowledge is not the secret possession of the few, but is acquired eventually from the kind of research which the group itself has just undertaken.

2. Another way to tread in the steps of the scholars, though at a distance, is to glimpse at the kind of thinking that gave rise to form criticism. Let each sub-group be given a common type of gospel narrative, with the assignment to break it down into its basic elements purely as a story. If the form selected is a healing miracle, for example, the group could analyse each as follows: Who was healed? What was he told to do? What did Jesus do exactly? What was the result? Was it immediate or delayed? How did the cured person react? How did the onlookers react? Did Jesus make any other use of the occasion? Or an example of Jesus talking with an individual might be taken; or a parable.

The written result of such a study (the leader will usually be wise to ask for written synopses of discussion) will be a set of tabulations, which try to set out the basic form or skeleton of the material. These tabulations can then be compared and corrected, and this exercise itself will give a seeking group all the discussion it needs. Moreover, it would give the members a certain objectivity in looking at incidents which are part of a believer's ingrained knowledge of the Bible; and valuable insights could be gained without having to accept by any means the ultimate conclusions which many form critics reached in their studies.

If there is sufficient interest in the group, and someone with an adequate initial knowledge to give the others a start in their research, other literary forms could be studied in much the same way – poetry, drama, proverbs, folk-tales, songs, riddles, oratory. Scripture has them all, and that group is rare which will take the time to study these forms in depth.

3. We know that Christian doctrines derive ultimately from the Bible. At some time or another, usually as a result of the pressure of critical events in the life of the Church rather than of leisurely decisions in the cloisters, Church fathers have been driven to safeguard basic principles of the faith by expressing them in carefully worded statements. The statements are not biblical in the sense that they are direct quotations from Scripture, but they do claim to express the great norms of biblical faith. We now know them in the form of creeds.

If, therefore, we were to set such a creed (Apostles', Nicene, or denominational statements of one kind or another) alongside extended passages containing New Testament doctrine, we may expect to find some correlation. It is not to be expected that any passage, not even the whole letter to the Romans, will lend support to every clause in the creed. But the student can expect to keep coming across scriptural themes which prompt him to say, 'Ah, this must be the kind of Scripture which led the Church to formulate *that* doctrine.' Each sub-group can be given the whole of the creed to set alongside their allotted section of Scripture; or they can be given only one credal clause and let loose on the whole of the Bible! In either case, let the leader be ready for a host of questions, some of them from bewildered minds. This is a magnificent exercise for sharpening the class's appreciation of doctrine and the difficulties that face anyone who seeks to present living narrative in cold, propositional terms.

The material being set against Scripture in this way need not be a formal statement. Individual people, in their reading of theological books, may come across a section which they would like the group to assess critically in the light of biblical theology. This could happen particularly when a controversial book comes out, or a divisive newspaper article. A group which regularly compares statements about religion and ethics soon comes to know Scripture better and appraise the statements more maturely.
4. The last suggestion under this heading is really an exercise for the gourmet, for the man and woman who believes that words are worth studying for their own sake. In some senses, however, it is the most important of the many exercises recommended in this book, because it tackles a fundamental question. If we believe that the Bible contains eternal truth for all generations, what is that truth? Can it be contained in words, and if so, in what words? Can we point to any particular statement of Scripture and say, 'That statement, *as it stands*, has a crystal-clear meaning, and that meaning will always be unambiguous and spirtually relevant to any generation in any place'?

The search for such statements has been a subject for exhaustive study for the writer, to great personal profit. The search was for simple sentences that (1) were capable of a constant application to all societies, (2) were spiritual, in that they had to do with a man's spirit rather than his mind and body, (3) were saving, in that they offered that man's spirit the possibility of wholesome change, (4) allowed only the clearest of meanings, devoid of figures of speech, ambiguous pronouns, etc.

Naturally, with such pedantic limitations, this brief could not help but disqualify the bulk of the New Testament! (about 92 per cent in all!) For instance, 'You are the salt of the earth' is inadequate, as 'you' refers to followers of Christ and not all people, and 'salt of the earth' is a metaphor which means a

72

thousand things to a thousand preachers. For the purposes of this study, 'I am the good shepherd' was set aside for similar reasons. Historical incidents are discounted except as the recounting of them contains a reflection or conclusion which could be applied throughout history. 'A man went down from Jerusalem to Jericho' may have been a historical truth, but it is not for us a saving truth. And so on, and so on.

In short, the exercise is to put the Bible through a literary sieve, discarding the temporary, the illustrative, the particular. The process is naturally open to question, as it seems to discount the bulk of Scripture from being universal truth, in the strict literary sense. Yet of course that is not the intention. All Scripture is needed to build up the total written story of 'that wonderful redemption, God's remedy for sin'; all Scripture has preachability, if we can find the right key to unlock it; its beauty and its power lie precisely in the figures and particularities of its language. But to interpret all this wealth, we must have the clue, and the clue must lie in some central core of truth.

To pursue the logic, that truth must be discoverable, and if we say that the Bible is the written record of God's revelation to man, then that discovery has to be made somewhere in the Bible. In order to preach the gospel we must know the gospel, and if that gospel is in the Bible, we must find it.

Nor is there any need to feel guilty about our search. Evangelists do not call the gospel 'full', 'four-square' for nothing. The astonishing thing is that, when shorn of all its ambiguities and colouring, the Bible *has* a residue of simple sentences which are complete and adequate. Complete because they are saying all that the whole Bible is saying in its most sublime and literary moments, as if all figures of speech have finally to come to rest in 'simple truth'. Adequate because there is no need to add any new doctrine to it to meet the ethical or religious demands of any age. When Christ said he was 'Omega', the last word, he apparently meant it.

This sustained defence of one study approach seems justified if only to persuade believers to hurl whatever methods they like at Scripture; it knows how to look after itself. They should not forget that, as Mary Lathbury put it in her hymn, God and his truths are to be sought *beyond* the sacred page'. The group should be quite sure of all this, should have discussed the whole concept thoroughly, before starting on this kind of study. In fact, it is doubtful whether a group would get very far with such an analytical approach unless they did understand, and broadly sympathise with, the aim. When they do get under way, however, they will probably appreciate the intellectual stimulus it gives. Students will want to outrun their master in this matter of applying rigid conditions to the passage under study, and will find reasons for reducing whole sections of rhetoric and exhortation to fragments of two or three sentences. There will be much wrangling about words, about what constitutes a figure of speech ('After all, every word is a figure of speech, isn't it?' is sure to be said by someone some time, and quite properly). Fine, fine, as long as the group looks long and reverently at the fragments that are left, that none might be lost.

Devotional Subjects   13

1. Assuming that group members are also regular worshippers, it would do no harm for them to look at the Bible from time to time as if they themselves were intending to preach from it. They would then appreciate the craft of the sermon from the other side, as it were. To look at Scripture from the point of view of its preachability is to make certain of its features temporarily more valuable than others.

Take, for example, Paul's letter to the Colossians. Reading it, the preacher would be on the look-out for phrases which are powerful, original or striking enough to stand as acceptable subjects in themselves. On and around them he can build his biblical edifice. In the case of Colossians, therefore, he might well mark the following: 'the graciousness of God' (1:6); 'active goodness' (1:10); 'the realm of light' (1:12); 'Christ's afflictions still to be endured' (1:24); 'a mature member of

Christ's body' (1:29); 'Christ's way of circumcision' (2:11); 'an air of wisdom' (2:23); 'garments that suit' (3:12); 'the secret of Christ' (4:3).

Then, of course, for some mystical reason, the preacher is on the look-out for 'threesomes', trilogies of thought on which he can hang his traditional three-part address. He may find three nouns:

faith . . . hope . . . love (1:4–5)
fortitude, patience and joy (1:11)
forced piety, self-mortification . . . severity to the body (2:23)

three adjectives:
dedicated . . . without blemish . . . innocent (1:22)
rooted . . . built . . . consolidated (2:7)

three verbs:
continue . . . come to . . . grasp (2:2)

or three prepositions:
in him . . . through him . . . for him (1:16)

The wise preacher will want to be able to say in a sentence essentially what he will be saying in half an hour. He will therefore be grateful for any comprehensive statement ready prepared for him, especially if it also contains conjunctions or other hinge-words which offer a ready breakdown into a logical sequence of sub-statements; as in the following examples.

1:9–10: 'We ask God (What?) that you may receive from him all wisdom and spiritual understanding (Why?) for full insight into his will (With what result?), so that your manner of life may be worthy of the Lord and entirely pleasing to him.'
1:21–22: '*Formerly* you were yourselves (a) estranged from God; (b) you were his enemies in heart and mind, and (c) your deeds were evil. *But now* by Christ's death in his body of flesh and blood God has reconciled you to himself, *so that* he

75

may present you before himself as (a) dedicated men, (b) without blemish and (c) innocent in his sight.'

These illustrations should be sufficient to indicate the method (which, incidentally, is a good public relations activity for any preacher). Again, it is a question of exercising the *mind* in spiritual affairs, and of having one's *heart* strengthened thereby. The method is classed as devotional, precisely because its main result is usually a devotional one. In a sense, people preach to themselves as they play the preacher's game.

2. A more direct devotional approach is to ask each member to carry a specific question in his mind as he begins to study the given passage. The question will directly concern his own life experience, his relationship with Christ. He reads Scripture to see if it will help him to evaluate the answer to the question, and he should be ready to share his answer frankly with the rest of the group. This kind of study is best undertaken individually, not in sub-groups, with plenty of time for reflection, and polite insistence on as much quietness as possible. The leader might prepare papers to hand round, with the questions on, or perhaps, more imaginatively, a sign or symbol suggesting the question.

This is the kind of question to take into study:

1) Is there anything in this passage which presents itself in a new way, or indeed is being read as if for the first time, bringing real mental illumination?

2) Is there anything which is difficult to understand, either because of the language it is phrased in, or because of the meaning it seems to imply?

3) Is there anything which is frankly challenging to the spirit, revealing deficiences in thought or behaviour? Anything, in brief, which compels the reader to say, 'If this is right, I am wrong'?

4) Is there anything which offers unprecedented hope, or overwhelming assurance? Anything, in brief, which compels the reader to say, 'If this is right, I am saved'?

5) Read the passage, and recall whether any part of it directly

evokes a personal spiritual memory – when one had finally to accept the truth of a particular challenge or promise; when any part of the passage began to live; when someone preached memorably on one of its texts; when one heard it read with real power; etc.

6) Try to read the passage as if it were being addressed to a group of people who were one body, not just a collection of individuals. Would any particular promise or command be seen in a different light if this was done? (This is a very difficult exercise, and only shows how far away many congregations are from a concept of the implications of 'the body of Christ'.)

7) Is there anything in the passage which, if obeyed faithfully, would demand a change in the corporate life of the congregation to which the group belongs – in its organisation, use of time, worship pattern, code of conduct, etc.?

Creative Subjects   14

Previous chapters have stressed the study value of approaching Scripture creatively, that is, with an emphasis on the use of other media such as music and drama, and using the imagination equally with the intellect. Here, too, this minority interest can be exploited, as suggested below:

1. Occasionally, it is worth asking the group to read a short passage (it is probably better, also, to use a well known passage) and try to answer unusual questions about it. For example:

a) Read a majestic passage (such as Isa. 35 or Rom. 8:31-39, or Rev. 21:1-6) and ask the group to state in turn what *colour* they associate with the words! The same question can then be extended, without further reading, about people's instinctive impressions of Bible characters, or whole books.

b) Similar passages could be used with a view to associating them with particular pieces of music, or types of music.

c) After reading a passage, ask the group to describe it in one word: a verb (what does it *do* to the reader?); a noun (what is the overall impression or effect?); an adjective (what is its overall atmosphere or mood?).

d) Naturally, such impressions as will be forthcoming from the group are highly subjective and probably only subconsciously felt. Some embarrassment will have to be overcome, and considerable prompting required of the unconditioned group. Yet it is astonishing how many interesting study leads can be opened up by such questioning, and how Scripture manages to stay central to the discussion. It will also be surprising to see what other suggestions arise out of the group – that people should try to associate passages with other senses such as smell or taste. The leader who is doubtful of such remote 'fishing trips' should reflect that one or two observations that may come from them are more likely to offer genuine leads into absorbing study than a whole shoal of conventional remarks, none of which show the faintest glimmer of new life.

e) If the group is reading a narrative, let members be asked to visualise the incident, and then describe it in some detail. People can later compare their mental pictures, try to produce a composite picture, and try even more to interpret the 'doctrinal' implications of their picture. The word 'doctrinal' is difficult to explain in this context, but it does appear that people's mental images of biblical incidents are usually coloured by their beliefs. For example, people have a composite, total view of Christ – character, appearance, attitude to people, and so on – and they will put this mental image into the centre of every incident they read about him. Their interpretation of each incident, and of the details in it, will therefore be conditioned by what they already believe about the central figure. If this is so, then discussion of the details of such incidents, even an imaginative reconstruction of the scene, will eventually lead to that belief being exposed, and, if necessary, challenged.

2. There is also a creative approach to the words of Scripture:

a) Consider the figures of speech in the study passage. See how far they can be replaced by up-to-date equivalents, modern analogies. Is there an industrial equivalent of the good shepherd? What is our counterpart of the light under a bushel, a smoking flax and a bruised reed (Isa. 42:3), the potter and the clay (Isa.

64:8)? Or can the figure really be improved upon? If not, what is there in this illustration, or metaphor, or parable, that makes for its continuing relevance?

b) Study the verbs used in a continuous passage (preferably a doctrinal section, a prophecy, a psalm); list them, to assist study by isolating them; then see if any accurate generalisations can be made about them. Are they powerful or commonplace? Do they conjure up visual images or sound images? And so on. This is the kind of creative approach which could lead a group quite naturally to recognise fundamental differences between Old and New Testament language, and also to appreciate the difference a knowledge of the inflections of the original languages can make to our understanding of the text.

c) Similarly, individual leaders will be able to see the relevance of studying other grammatical forms – nouns, adjectives, adverbs, etc. The object of the study would be to see how the writers, as literary people, get their effects, wherein lies their power and persuasiveness quite apart from the intrinsic importance of the message. That message can only be enhanced by such study, never detracted from.

Such could be said for all the fragmentary studies recommended here. By concentrating on a tiny facet of the whole, and working at that facet with industry and care, the student is by way of being 'faithful in that which is least'. In this case, the reward is a happier understanding of that which is greatest.

6
True-to-Life Studies

15

Sooner or later, as must be agreed, all Scripture must be brought to the acid test – does it work in real life? Are its eternal, spiritual truths such as can be relied upon and put into practice by the ordinary person? Did the Bible writers know all about life when they gave us these noble standards of behaviour, or were they theorising like philosophers?

Of course, that is not to say that the only test of Scripture is whether or not *we* can believe it, or find that *we* can live up to it. We should humbly accept that revealed truth is a better guide than our own life experience of compromise and half-thought. We study Scripture precisely in order to correct our personal prejudices and misconceptions against the yardstick of truth.

But that truth has to *be* truth. There is little point, for instance, in Paul asserting that 'all alike have sinned', if we could immediately pop into town and find a couple of thousand people who demonstrably had not sinned. There is no comfort at all in the promises of God if they are not kept, and no incentive to keep their conditions if there is no possibility of keeping them, simply because we are human.

At some point, therefore, we have a right to take the truths of Scripture as we find them, and hurl at them every objection we can find. Alternatively, we can draw on every corner of our communal experience, and support or question the claims of the Bible. Our last worry should be whether or not the texts can stand up to scrutiny. We are more likely to realise first, either that we did not really understand what the text is saying, or that the Bible is even truer than ever the preachers tell us.

There will be adverse reaction to this approach on the part of some. 'Have we a right to treat the Holy Bible like this? If Jesus said anything, for instance, it must be right, simply because he said it; what is there therefore to discuss? We can seek to understand, but we can't question.' And so on. This fair argument is an occupational hazard for leaders of discussions, and the objections carry some weight.

None the less, a sincere and responsive group will soon see that the way of the questioning mind is another authentic approach to Bible study. It needs one or two safeguards built into it, and these will be pointed out later. But it may well prove to be an approach which stimulates more real thinking about spiritual issues, and more ultimate faith in the Bible, than any other so far discussed. The method is simply to take a Bible text *as it stands* and test its relevance and value to the group by asking a specific kind of question. The examples given below are of several groups of texts, each with one factor in common. Where there is extended time for study discussion, the whole set of texts can be studied at one sitting. As likely as not, however, the group will get engrossed in one, at most two, texts, so the sets given may also be taken as subjects for whole series of discussions. Each set is preceded here by the kind of question which is likely to stimulate discussion.

1. Are we completely sure that we have understood New Testament ethics? What place do we find in our thinking about behaviour, for such texts as these?

God is greater than our conscience. (1 John 3:20)
Although all wrongdoing is sin, not all sin is deadly sin. (1 John 5:17)
Love cancels innumerable sins. (1 Pet. 4:8)
Anything which does not arise from conviction is sin. (Rom. 14:23)

2. How far can we identify ourselves with some of the clear words of Scripture with respect to particular points of behaviour? Are there extenuating circumstances, or are we bound to follow them literally?

Do not turn your back on a man who wants to borrow. (Matt. 5:42)
Every person must submit to the supreme authorities. (Rom. 13:1)
You also ought to wash one another's feet. (John 13:14)
Use your worldly wealth to win friends for yourselves. (Luke 16:9)

3. Are the following observations about men true? Or do they need some clarification or amendment? (Do not be content with a first-thought judgement; probe the texts from all sides, leaving no aspect of life and behaviour unconsidered.)

A man reaps what he sows. (Gal. 6:7)
The man who never says a wrong thing is a perfect character. (Jas. 3:2)
A man's anger cannot promote the justice of God. (Jas. 1:20)
The man who is dishonest in little things is dishonest also in great things. (Luke 16:10)
Religion does yield high dividends, but only to the man whose resources are within him. (1 Tim. 6:6)
If a man does not know how to control his own family, how can he look after a congregation of God's people? (1 Tim. 3:5)
Every man who does right is (God's) child. (1 John 2:29)

4. Not all Christians would accept the following statements unreservedly, because, of their traditions. What does the group make of them?

The prayer offered in faith will save the sick man. (Jas. 5:15)
A man gifted with the Spirit can judge the worth of everything, but is not himself subject to judgment by his fellowmen. (Cor. 2:15)

If you forgive any man's sins, they stand forgiven; if you pronounce them unforgiven, unforgiven they remain. (John 20:23)

Nothing that goes into a man from outside can defile him. (Mark 7:15)

If a man keeps the whole law apart from one single point, he is guilty of breaking all of it. (Jas. 2:10)

A child of God does not commit sin; he cannot be a sinner. (1 John 3:9)

5. Entering the area of personal experience, how far can the individual group member identify himself with the 'I' in the following texts? What reservations must be made?

I have learned to find resources in myself whatever my circumstances. (Phil. 4:11)

I have sinned against God ... and am no longer fit to be called ... son. (Luke 15:21)

I have strength for anything through him who gives me power. (Phil. 4:13)

Everyone else may fall away on your account, but I never will. (Matt. 26:33)

I have been crucified with Christ. (Gal. 2:20)

6. To what extent have individuals in the group, or the group as a group, had confirmation of these general statements in their own experience?

In everything, as we know, [the Spirit] co-operates for good with those who love God. (Rom. 8:28)

Persecution will come to all who want to live a godly life as Christians. (2 Tim. 3:12)

The wound which is borne in God's way brings a change of heart too salutary to regret. (2 Cor. 7:10)

Disputing about mere words ... does no good, and it is the ruin of those who listen. (2 Tim. 2:14)

You will have ample means in yourselves to meet each and

every situation, with enough and to spare for every good cause. (2 Cor. 9:8)

There is nothing ... that can separate us from the love of God. (Rom. 8:39)

The Spirit comes to the aid of our weakness. (Rom. 8:26)

7. How far is each individual really sure of the implications or promise behind these statements about God? Do we ever tend to act contrary to these beliefs?

Your Father who sees what is done in secret will reward you. (Matt. 6:4)

He has chosen things low and contemptible, mere nothings, to overthrow the existing order. (1 Cor. 1:28)

The gracious gifts of God and his calling are irrevocable. (Rom. 11:29)

God has no favourites. (Eph. 6:9; Rom. 2:11)

All good giving, every perfect gift, comes from above, from the Father of the lights of heaven. (Jas. 1:17)

8. Philosophise on the rightness or otherwise of the following:

Nothing is impure in itself. (Rom. 14:14)

Nothing is altogether soundless. (1 Cor. 14:10)

It follows that as the issue of one misdeed was condemnation for all men, so the issue of one just act is acquittal and life for all men. (Rom. 5:18)

Where there is no law there can be no breach of law. (Rom. 4:15)

If the whole were one single organ, there would not be a body at all. (1 Cor. 12:19)

The perishable cannot possess immortality. (1 Cor. 15:50)

What is seen passes away; what is unseen is eternal. (2 Cor. 4:18)

The whole created universe groans in all its parts as if in the pangs of childbirth. (Rom. 8:22)

The love of money is the root of all evil things. (1 Tim. 6:10)
Good deeds ... cannot be concealed for ever. (1 Tim. 5:25)

9. Study the different meanings of the same English word in the following text sequences and come to some conclusions about the biblical concepts conveyed by such words:

(a) *flesh* (RSV)
They went into the ark ... two and two of all flesh. (Gen. 7:15)
You are my bone and my flesh. (2 Sam. 19:12)
... who walk not according to the flesh, but according to the spirit. (Rom. 8:4)
To remain in the flesh is more necessary on your account. (Phil. 1:24)
(b) *faith* (RSV)
We are justified by faith. (Rom. 5:1)
I have kept the faith. (2 Tim. 4:7)
Can his faith save (man)? (Jas. 2:14)
Faith is the assurance of things hoped for. (Heb. 11:1)

Many more words can be sorted out from a concordance, or from several theological wordbooks. In each case, the study procedure will be to define the key word as it is used in any one of the texts, see whether the same word can sustain the same meaning in the next text, and study how far one has to keep modifying the original definition.

There is no doubt that productive discussion could follow on a consideration of texts along the lines suggested in this chapter. There is equally no doubt that such activity needs an essential corrective if it is to deserve the name of a study discussion. Almost every one of these texts must be related back to its context so that people may know what exactly the text is trying to say. This relating to context may be done at the beginning, to prevent misconceptions from developing, or later, when people have exhausted themselves of their own interpretations and have reached the stage where they badly want some clarification. If it is not done at any time, all that has happened is that a group of individuals has had a general 'religious' discussion which happened to start with a quotation from the Bible. If it *is* done, people are induced to learn how to look at Scripture as a whole.

One example will serve to point what must be an obvious moral. One might start with the text, 'Perfect love banishes fear' (1 John 4:18). Now a critical look at this text, from the point of view of human experience, will quickly show that in fact most Christians must frankly admit that they have some fears still in their make-up. They may be afraid of heights, closed or open spaces, darkness, water, etc. They may be afraid of particular things happening to them in the future – blindness, widowhood, and so on. They may be physically cowardly, or temperamentally shy and fearful of people's reactions and criticism.

When the group has admitted to this host of fears and complexes, the leader of the study may then ask, 'Have we got to say then that those of us who have such fears cannot at the same time be knowing "perfect love"?' There will be those people who are ever ready to bring themselves down, and will agree that they lack love (or faith, or hope), and that these things might disappear if they had greater love. On the other hand, people might question the other part of the text, and ask what is really meant by fear. If fear means these kinds of fear, then either Christians in general do not have the love (in which case why does God write out a promise cheque which no one can cash, as it were?), or else this statement is a false one, and does not relate to life.

This is probably the moment to look at the whole context of the quotation (v. 16–19). Then it becomes clear (which is rarely pointed out in sermons) that he who 'dwells in love' (towards God and therefore, as the whole letter continually points out, towards man) need not be plagued with the specific *fear of being condemned by God*. He can face the fact of judgment precisely because he is obeying the conditions of the judgment. So this is not a thoughtless blanket statement which seems to make a 'proper' Christian immune from all manner of fears and complexes. It is a more limited, but no less liberating, statement that the man who truly loves can be confident of his essential acceptance with God, and need not fret about it.

Such an example should confirm that this kind of contextual study is necessary in most if not all cases, if the group wishes to engage in true study.

There is a refinement of the method which may appeal to some groups, and which would place an even greater study premium on the whole activity. Try to have a discussion about a text during which, at least for the first few minutes, participants are only allowed to speak if they offer some specific Scripture from elsewhere which can throw light on the meaning of the text in question. At this stage, that is, they are not allowed to take a personal view. Some of the supportive Scripture advanced will be quite irrelevant, but there is no need to embarrass contributors by saying this, as later discussion will act as a natural sieve. The initial discipline will test the group's ability, first of all to retain Scripture, then, more importantly, to relate one part of it to another. It will not always be a case of reciting texts. People may support a New Testament text with an Old Testament incident, or give a personal appraisal of a particular biblical theme or emphasis.

This is true synthetic study, the bringing together of thoughts separated in time and situation so as to bring light to bear on a single theme. Which, of course, is the basic study objective of the approach described throughout this chapter.

7

Exposition and Discussion

16

Behind the practical approaches outlined in this book has been the implicit claim that the Bible itself is in no way to blame for the apathy which too often surrounds its study in a group context. The fault lies rather with our tradition of approaching its study with limited and in some ways difficult tools. We have relied upon the ability of individuals to expound Scripture to others, upon the ability of groups to engage in purposeful discussion, and on a strong, unstimulated desire on the part of everyone to study in the first place. It is precisely these assets that are generally in short supply in most modern congregations. It seemed right, therefore, to attempt to suggest other tools and methods which might depend rather less on these scarce commodities.

Of course, 'when that which is perfect is come', and those same advantages are in fact to hand, something really vital and authentic presents itself. Aids, experiments, activities, all the paraphernalia of teaching techniques, have a habit of looking a little naïve and forced when a real teacher is around, one who carries the power of a thousand gimmicks in his own person. All methods and suggestions fall away, and rightly so, if you have (a) a genuine desire to understand the Bible, and (b) someone whom the group accepts as capable of helping them to that understanding. To put it ideally, if every congregation had a Gamaliel, all that would remain would be to sit at his feet and listen.

Then, and perhaps only then, what has been termed here as 'conventional' Bible study would come into its own as the best and simplest group method of study – reasoned, illuminating exposition by one man, followed by perceptive discussion on the part of everyone else; with perhaps a devotional epilogue, allowing everyone to marvel at the new light shed once again on and by God's word. This much is freely admitted, as it was in the introduction to this book, and none of the other suggestions in this book can better the plain devotional exposition in the hands of the man or woman who 'knows'.

Nevertheless, the ghosts of Sangster, Campbell Morgan and the like do not lurk in every company of Bible students, and most of us who take up the direct expositional approach are wearing armour which is too big. The faithful may respond – those who are stimulated to study in any case and can incredibly see past the words to the Word – but there is little hope of engaging the presence, or thereafter the attention, of the uncommitted who form the bulk of most unrenewed congregations.

Having sounded this warning (perhaps too often and too pessimistically for some readers), some thought could be given to improving one's approach to the exposition-discussion type of study. While admitting personal limitations with respect to Bible exposition, many leaders will probably still feel reluctant to follow any other than the known path in this respect. They may feel that, though in principle they can see the excitement and benefit of other approaches, they would have to make their own cautious experiments only within a pattern which they recognise as familiar. This is understandable, and it may be the reaction of the group as well as the teacher. Yet, when following the talk-chat approach, it is still important to ask oneself questions such as: 'Are we taking these studies seriously enough, as students as well as worshippers? Are there any adjustments we could make to our programme which might bring about a real improvement?'

For instance, too many groups have settled too easily for their low membership, assuming that what is now ever shall be. This kind of defeatist spirit has a habit of communicating itself to those outside. Any group which accepts the role of an inevitable minority, a remnant, a cul-de-sac, has given itself a handicap when it comes to attracting new membership. By contrast, the programme could be advertised to the congregation at large; positive and confident personal invitation can be practised; groups have been known to devise printed invitations. One could well argue that a study group, however healthy, might always, even of *theological* necessity, be only a small section of the total congregation. Even so, the important thing is not to convey the impression that it exists as a kind of scapegoat, undergoing a sacrificial labour of love on behalf of the rest of the community, which may therefore go on its way guiltless. If this is how the group does see itself, the rest of the congregation will undoubtedly let it rest in peace.

Has the existing group a progressive plan of action for the future, or does it tend to live week by week from hand to mouth, as if consciously living in the last days? Take, for example, the question of equipment. There is no reason why groups should not build up communal resources like most other 'clubs' do, that is if they intend to carry on over the years.

Most groups would benefit greatly from having a small library of reference books available at the place where the study is held. A concordance (preferably more than one copy), at least two different one-volume commentaries, a Bible atlas, a Bible dictionary, a Bible handbook, a theological wordbook, a variety of translations and paraphrases, and a sufficient quantity of Bibles (in the translation which has been accepted as standard by the group) to have on hand for the visitor or new member. Given such a library, the next thing is to make sure that it is used. Take time to make sure that each member of the class understands the separate functions of each reference book, and institute a regular procedure by which the appropriate book is quickly but surely referred to with the minimum of delay.

The go-ahead group may even wish to purchase the occasional bigger and dearer teaching aid such as wall map, cassette, filmstrip; or subscribe to a suitable periodical; or take upon itself the job of creating and maintaining a small devotional library on behalf of the whole congregation. The occasional group has been known to supply the total congregation with an occasional duplicated report of its more positive discussions.

Anything is better than the feeling of impermanence which pervades many groups. A feeling which is not helped by some of the seating arrangements which groups tolerate. Much research has taken place in recent years (e.g. when planning new buildings) concerning the creative use of space and the effect that this has on groups using that space. Such findings often show that virtually the least productive way for a small group to occupy space, if it wishes to create an atmosphere of relaxed sharing, is to sit in short, tight rows one behind the other, or to scatter aimlessly over a large space. By some irony, these appear to be the favoured, or at least the accepted, arrangements for class and congregation. Things have probably improved in this respect over the last decade, but it still too often needs a conscious and persistent effort to persuade people to take up other formations – the circle, a semi-circle, informal seating in a restricted area, small tables to write on, etc. When groups gravitate to private houses, as they appear to be doing more and more, such seating arrangements become natural and even compulsory. It is in halls that the intimate touch must be worked for; not to bother is to give oneself an unnecessary disability from the start.

To return to another aspect of equipment, leaders who prefer the straight approach to Bible study should consider the greater use of the effective study-aids which exist to further that precise approach. Extensive book lists could be added to this chapter, yet they may not be used so very much, because of a curious inertia which settles on groups. It is as if they are resolved to prove G. K. Chesterton right in a way which he never intended when he said, 'If a thing is worth doing at all, it is worth doing badly.'!

A leader may admit his limitations as an exponent of Scripture; he may also admit his reluctance or inability to try other ways of studying; but, in fairness to his group,·he should go on to admit that he needs to seek help if he is to persist with a method which relies so heavily on his exposition. One has only to walk into a Christian bookshop to see the variety of study aids which must still largely be untried by the majority of students. There are leaflets, pamphlets, booklets, offering basic material for study programmes, with questions for group discussion and personal written follow-up – often by well-known scholars. There are work books for adult students, showing how best to approach different kinds of Scripture. There are information sheets and cards, pamphlets on all manner of related subjects – Bible archaeology, the formation of the New Testament canon, etc. These are all aspects of study which the methods described in this book do not stress at all. But if they are taken up, let them be taken up properly; and let the leader of the orthodox Bible study take hold of what orthodoxy waits to put into his hands. To be 'professional' has been defined simply as taking things seriously. In this striking sense of the word, all Bible classes should be professional.

One fact above all must be remembered by any who take on the challenge of leading others to learn, by whatever method. This is that learning has its laws; a man or a woman acquires knowledge by definite processes. The laws are not man made, though they may have been recognised and codified by him; they are part of the nature of things, of man himself. They have also to be obeyed, knowingly or otherwise, before even the keenest mind can add to its real knowledge.

For example, much Christian education has been ineffective because it has relied on the strange assumption that somehow the Bible teaches itself, just because it is the Bible. It was this aura that kept people from seeing Scripture as literature in the straightforward sense of the word for so long. It seemed as if its claim to contain inspired truth for all time could only be upheld as long as it was not subject to critical scrutiny.

Many of the arrogant results of this illogic have been largely set aside by now, but one aspect of it is as powerful as ever. In the mind of many Bible teachers lurks a dangerous piece of logic. Put simply, it goes like this: 'We are going to study the Bible, therefore Christians, people who "believe" the Bible, must automatically be interested in studying it.' According to this argument, the facts that Scripture really does have in it those truths for which man's spirit pines, and that most Christians have a strong sense that they *ought* to be interested, are adequate incentives for study, without the need to engage any other kind of interest. This kind of argument also leads to the many sub-myths which surround the Bible as a thing in itself – that it cannot be helped on its healing way by any of man's achievements in the realm of mind or spirit, that its truths are talismans for the believer, that 'to lift up Christ' means to repeat often enough a small body of evangelical texts, that people are consciously 'crying out for the gospel'.

All the history and theory of teaching suggests the contrary. That vital part of a man which he must hand over before he can learn – his interest – is not surrendered lightly, and certainly not at the behest of a mindless authoritarian approach which commands, 'Be interested!' This 'interest' is an illusive thing. A man may give his attention, as when he pauses to listen to a speaker on a street corner, without necessarily giving his committed interest also. Or that attention may be real but short lived, and thereafter he may give only his apparent attention. This is one of the acceptable deceits of the adult world, and many worshippers would have to admit that, despite their Sunday faces, 'their thoughts remain below'. A man may respond warmly to humour, and too many preachers have been content with this hollow victory, thinking they have got their man, whereas their man was as far as ever from being really engaged in his mind.

No, a man's interest – that almost indefinable commitment which makes him want to search and think, not once but a second and a third time – that kind of interest must be angled for, mined, gained by stealth. Keys in the mind have to be turned, by design or accident, before a man will even consent to learn. He may want to learn Scripture for its own sake, may feel guilty that he doesn't know it better, may be drawn irresistibly to it. Yet he may have to turn away disappointed time and again because the leader of his study could not make things 'click' for him. These are harsh words, because they put a clear burden on the leader of a Bible study to exercise teaching talent on behalf of his group and not rely on the spiritual power of his subject to move mental mountains. They may also sound heretical words, because they suggest that the transfer of divine truth can be held up by the inefficiency of human teachers. Well, we must accept that possibility, and tremble.

This whole argument could be stated another way, perhaps more acceptably. It is clear, both from the Bible and from life, that a man can gain spiritual insight without having to acquire factual knowledge. This is as well for most of us. To know true conversion, for instance, a man does not need to know the various Greek words for 'salvation', or the exact itinerary of Paul's journeys, or the history of Temple sacrifices. When people rejoice in 'a simple faith', they are usually saying that their personal acquaintance with Christ came about, and is maintained, without having to come to grips with the problems and facts which an intellectual search demands. This is eminently so, and by the same token, even those who must keep searching, by virtue of their temperament or their profession, are wise to keep their own simplicities intact. 'The things of the Spirit of God . . . are spiritually discerned.'

However, when a man does desire to acquire historical or theological facts, he must acquire them through his *mind*; he cannot acquire them spiritually or intuitively. If he is ever to sort out the respective histories of Judah and Israel, or the teaching on the Second Coming, or the Pauline view of the Church, he can only do so by having a strong enough interest and a lively enough mind to actually learn about them. No amount of spiritual power, 'better part' as it certainly is, can present him with facts unbidden and unsought. The inspiration of Scripture does not include that kind of inspiration which is willing to short-circuit the normal processes of learning and present a man clairvoyantly with all the facts he wants. It is possible to perceive by nature the *spirit* of Scripture, as Paul argued in Romans on behalf of the Gentiles; but it is not possible to perceive the *content* of Scripture in the same way. To know the Bible one must read it and must think about it.

One must therefore also be helped to think about it, and so we return to the obligation of the Christian teacher. And this digression has sought to underline the most serious criticism to be levelled against much Bible study – it defies the laws of learning. The activity which was genuinely meant to encourage study is too often the very act which most discourages it. Some of the wasted effort of the teacher will be saved if he bears in mind the humble corrective that a teacher cannot teach anyone. The best he can do, all he can aim to do, is to create a situation in which people can learn. People will learn when, and not until, they can add a new concept or fact to the concepts and facts which they already have, in a way which makes sense to *them*. Anything less than this – listening to torrents of words, however true, but for which they can see no relevance, feel no quickening – is not learning. It is a teacher talking, or acting, on an unconscious ego trip, or whatever.

One more cautionary word. The suggestion that teaching is regrettably much more common than learning will also help to explain why many Christian congregations 'sit at the feet' of ministers for years without ever really progressing in wisdom, either factual or spiritual. The probability is that the teaching, though frequent, has actually been repetitive over a very limited area, and that there has really been very little new to learn week by week. This danger was spelled out to Christian congregations in New Testament times: 'Though by this time you ought to be teachers, you need someone to teach you the ABC of God's oracles over again ... Let us then stop discussing the rudiments of Christianity. We ought not to be laying over again the foundations of faith in God ... Instead, let us advance towards maturity.' (Heb. 5: 12-6.3)

In Bible class terms, this means that the leader, if he is responsible for a class over a period of years, must teach systematically and broadly, not staying only with themes that suit him personally. It is sad when middle-aged Christians of long standing are still fumbling for reasoned attitudes of faith when *one* informed look at Scripture could have resolved those attitudes years ago. We bear needless pain, and forfeit peace, quite as much by abstaining from Bible study as from prayer. Scripture will provide any man of faith, however intelligent and introspective, with at least a launching-pad on which to rest his thoughts about any real issue of life. The leader must point people to such foundations, and help them more and more to discover that Scripture has 'its use for teaching the truth and refuting error, or for reformation of manners and discipline in right living.' (2 Tim. 3:16).

It is right that this book should end by putting the onus solidly on the leader of the Bible study, not the group itself. In one way this is not right nor true, because the Bible is there for the taking by the individual believer, who must be ultimately responsible for his own response to the opportunity. The Spirit of God is still the best informer of minds and purifier of hearts. Yet the charge to the teacher is justified in the context of this book, which has been basically for people who have proposed themselves for this kind of leadership. They must not be let off the hook in the final paragraph! We know that the Holy Spirit has the last word, but we must work and prepare as if he had not, as if all depended on our personal fidelity and ability. We must avoid the immature moan that we have piped for people and they would not dance – all we might be saying is that our personal playing technique was just not up to it. If the tune is an eternal one, pleasant to every ear that hears it clearly; and if the instinct to dance to that tune is implanted in every heart, as we believe, then we must keep playing till we play properly and men's spirits leap with excitement. Paul knew all about it, as his letters testify (AV): 'Though I be free from all men, yet have I made myself servant unto all, that I might gain the more . . . I am made all things to all men, so that I might *by all means* save some. And this I do for the gospel's sake.'